YO-AAF-913

Bibliography on Soviet Intelligence and Security Services

Westview Special Studies

The concept of Westview Special Studies is a response to the continuing crisis in academic and informational publishing. Library budgets are being diverted from the purchase of books and used for data banks, computers, micromedia, and other methods of information retrieval. Interlibrary loan structures further reduce the edition sizes required to satisfy the needs of the scholarly community. Economic pressures on university presses and the few private scholarly publishing companies have greatly limited the capacity of the industry to properly serve the academic and research communities. As a result, many manuscripts dealing with important subjects, often representing the highest level of scholarship, are no longer economically viable publishing projects--or, if accepted for publication, are typically subject to lead times ranging from one to three years.

Westview Special Studies are our practical solution to the problem. As always, the selection criteria include the importance of the subject, the work's contribution to scholarship, and its insight, originality of thought, and excellence of exposition. We accept manuscripts in camera-ready form, typed, set, or word processed according to specifications laid out in our comprehensive manual, which contains straightforward instructions and sample pages. The responsibility for editing and proofreading lies with the author or sponsoring institution, but our editorial staff is always available to answer questions and provide guidance.

The result is a book printed on acid-free paper and bound in sturdy library-quality soft covers. We manufacture these books ourselves using equipment that does not require a lengthy make-ready process and that allows us to publish first editions of 300 to 1000 copies and to reprint even smaller quantities as needed. Thus, we can produce Special Studies quickly and can keep even very specialized books in print as long as there is a demand for them.

About the Book and Authors

Literature in English and Russian on the Soviet intelligence and security services has grown rapidly over the last 40 years. This annotated bibliography is a valuable tool for research and teaching on Soviet intelligence and its role in the country's domestic and international affairs. The authors, working under the auspices and with the assistance of the Consortium for the Study of Intelligence, have categorized and annotated nearly 500 books, articles, and government documents pertaining to Soviet intelligence.

Raymond G. Rocca is a former senior intelligence official of the Central Intelligence Agency and was adjunct professor at the Defense Intelligence College. John J. Dziak is a senior Soviet specialist at the Defense Intelligence Agency and adjunct professor at George Washington University.

Bibliography on Soviet Intelligence and Security Services

Raymond G. Rocca
and John J. Dziak
with the staff of the Consortium for
the Study of Intelligence

Westview Press / Boulder and London

A Westview Special Study

Spelling inconsistencies are due to variation in transliterations. Whenever
possible, Board of Geographic Names spellings are used.

Published in Cooperation with the Consortium for the Study of Intelligence

All rights reserved. No part of this publication may be reproduced or trans-
mitted in any form or by any means, electronic or mechanical, including
photocopy, recording, or any information storage and retrieval system, without permission in writing from the publisher.

Copyright © 1985 by National Strategy Information Center, Inc., except for
Frontispiece, copyright © 1984 by John J. Dziak and Raymond G. Rocca, and
Chart, copyright © 1985 by John J. Dziak and Raymond G. Rocca

Published in 1985 in the United States of America by Westview Press, Inc.;
Frederick A. Praeger, Publisher; 5500 Central Avenue, Boulder, Colorado 80301

Library of Congress Cataloging in Publication Data
Rocca, Raymond
    Bibliography on Soviet intelligence and security
services.
    (Westview special study)
    1. Secret service--Soviet Union--Bibliography.
2. Intelligence service--Soviet Union--Bibliography.
I. Dziak, John. II. Title.
Z6724.I7R6 1985 [UB251.S65] 016.3271'2'0947 85-3257
ISBN: 0-8133-7048-5

Composition for this book was provided by the Consortium for the Study of
Intelligence
Printed and bound in the United States of America

10 9 8 7 6 5 4 3 2 1

Contents

Foreword

In the late 1970's scholarly research and teaching in the United States about intelligence-related subjects increased dramatically. Since that time, intelligence has evolved into a new teaching and research field not only in the US but also in the United Kingdom and Canada. A principal reason for this development was the expanded volume of information on intelligence available to scholars and policy specialists. This was, in part, the result of the writings of former intelligence officials, materials derived from Congressional oversight, and documents released under the Freedom of Information Act. Additionally, intelligence became an important public policy issue and the subject of scholarly investigation.

In 1979 growing academic interest in intelligence led to the establishment of the Consortium for the Study of Intelligence (CSI) under the auspices by the National Strategy Information Center (NSIC). For twenty years, NSIC--a nonpartisan tax-exempt educational institution--has initiated and sponsored scholarly research and teaching on national security-related subjects. The Consortium for the Study of Intelligence has extended this work to the study and teaching of intelligence as it relates to national security, foreign policy, law and ethics.

Founding members included faculty from major universities and public policy research centers throughout the US. The purpose of the Consortium was to provide an institutional forum for researchers and practitioners interested in intelligence studies. The Consortium has sponsored seven major research colloquia as well as numerous seminars for university teachers interested in intelligence studies.

As part of its research into intelligence theory, the Consortium has stressed not only the study of US intelligence practices, but also that of other major contemporary intelligence systems as well. One which has received attention both in the US and abroad is the Soviet system. The literature on the Soviet intelligence and security services in English and Russian has expanded dramatically over the last 40 years. While the volume of research and publications continues to grow, it is difficult for scholars and policy analysts to ascertain what materials are available and which may be most helpful. This annotated Bibliography on Soviet Intelligence and Security Services begins to address these concerns by providing an analytic aid for research and teaching about Soviet intelligence and its role in both Soviet domestic politics and contemporary world affairs. The bibliography likewise will be helpful for those engaged in comparative intelligence studies and hopefully will be followed by annotated bibliographies on the intelligence and security services of other States.

Over five hundred books, articles, and Congressional and other documents on Soviet intelligence have been categorized into five sections: Selected Bibliographies and other reference works, Russian/ Soviet Accounts (many available in English translation), Defector/First-Hand Accounts, Secondary Accounts, and Congressional and other government documents. Some of the sections are further divided to separate books, and articles and other short works. Writings on Soviet Bloc services are not treated as separate categories but are subsumed under the appropriate Soviet sections. Of special note are citations from Congressional testimony by defectors. These Congressional documents provide information and analysis which often is not found in published memoirs. The materials contained herein have been drawn from a wide variety of sources. Whenever appropriate the US edition or the English language edition has been cited first. Additional publication data have been included when they may be of special interest. Following many of the citations is a brief annotation.

The citations and annotations were compiled by two specialists in Soviet intelligence who have had both extensive experience in the US government and have also taught the subject for many years. Mr. Raymond Rocca is a former senior intelligence official of the Central Intelligence Agency and was an adjunct Professor at the Defense Intelligence College. Dr. John J. Dziak is a senior official at the Defense Intelligence

Agency and adjunct Professor at George Washington University's Institute for Sino-Soviet Studies.

Assisting in the research and technical support in preparation of the bibliography were members of the Washington office staff of the National Strategy Information Center with special thanks to Christine Thompson, Mary Hartigan, and Timothy Campbell.

Roy Godson
Consortium for the
Study of Intelligence
and
Georgetown University

Section One

Selected Bibliographies and Other Reference Works

1.   BLACKSTOCK, Paul W. and F.L. SCHAF Jr., eds.

     INTELLIGENCE, ESPIONAGE, COUNTERESPIONAGE AND COVERT OPERATIONS: A GUIDE TO INFORMATION SOURCES

     Detroit, Michigan: Gale Research Co., 1978, pp. 255.

An annotated general intelligence bibliography, organized by subject category. Numerous entries are included on the Soviet security and intelligence services; see pp. 20-23, 97-104, 149-155, 169-171, 219, and 224.

2.   CLINE, Majorie W., Carla E. CHRISTIANSEN and Judith M. FONTAINE, eds.

     SCHOLAR'S GUIDE TO INTELLIGENCE LITERATURE: BIBLIOGRAPHY OF THE RUSSEL J. BOWEN COLLECTION, GEORGETOWN UNIVERSITY

     Frederick, Maryland: University Publications of America, Inc., 1983, pp. 236; published for the National Intelligence Study Center.

Unannotated, but many headings of this topically arranged survey of the literature deal with the Soviet services. See "National Intelligence Establishments", pp. 5-7; "Collection of Information", pp. 25-6, 38-9, 45-7; "Counterintelligence", pp. 59-61, 69-75; "Assassinations", pp. 103, 105; "Foreign Relations", pp. 116-7; "Political Dissent", p. 121; "Psychological Warfare", pp. 124-5; "Unconventional Warfare", p. 136; "Wars", pp. 153-6, 163, 172, 183.

3.   CONSTANTINIDES, George C.

**INTELLIGENCE AND ESPIONAGE: AN ANALYTICAL
BIBLIOGRAPHY**

Boulder, Colorado: Westview Press, 1983, pp. 559.

A select, annotated general bibliography of intelligence literature. Arranged alphabetically, it
includes: Intelligence Category Index; Annotated List
of Entries by Author; Glossary and Abbreviations; Title
Index; and Subject and Author Index. A limited number
of entries on the Soviet services.

4.   DEFENSE INTELLIGENCE COLLEGE, **Bibliography of
Intelligence Literature,** Washington, D.C.: Defense
Intelligence College, 1985, 8th Edition, pp. 90.

Annotated entries are listed alphabetically by author.
About a fourth of the items concern or relate to Soviet
security and intelligence organization and operations.

5.   DEPARTMENT OF DEFENSE, Department of the Army,
Area Handbook for the Soviet Union, 1971, (Washington DC, GPO), pp. 827.

Produced under contract (DA Pam 550-95) by The
American University, Foreign Area Studies Division.

Balanced, though now outdated. See, "The State Security
System", Chapter 7, pp. 119-137; "The Internal Security
System", Chapter 8, pp. 139-156; "The Legal System",
Chapter 22, pp 441-470; and "The Police (Militia) and
Correctional Systems", Chapter 23, pp. 471-486.

6.   DEPARTMENT OF DEFENSE, **Lexicon of Selected Soviet
Terms Relating to Maskirovka,** (Deception),
DDB-2460-3-83. (1983).

A specialized dictionary of terms relating to Soviet
military deception including disinformation, camouflage, diversion, and simulation.

7.   FLORINSKY, Michael T., ed.

THE McGRAW-HILL ENCYCLOPEDIA OF RUSSIA AND THE
SOVIET UNION

New York, New York: McGraw-Hill, 1961, pp. 624.

Contributions on Soviet state security organization and
personalities by recognized specialists. See entries:
"Intelligence", pp. 245-47 and "Security Police", pp.
502-504.

8.   GRIERSON, Philip

BOOKS ON SOVIET RUSSIA, 1917-1942: A BIBLIOGRAPHY
AND A GUIDE TO READING

London, England: Metheuen and Co. Ltd., 1943,
pp. 354.

Reprinted: Twickenham, England: Anthony C. Hall,
1969.

The leading annotated bibliography for the period
covered. See "The Secret Police, Concentration Camps
and the Great Trials", pp. 120-130 and "The Third
International (Comintern)", pp. 131-151.

9.   GUNZENHAUSER, Max

GESCHICHTE DES GEHEIMEN NACHRICHTENDIENSTES
(SPIONAGE, SABOTAGE UND ABWHER)

[History of Secret Intelligence Services (Espionage, Sabotage and Counterintelligence)]

Frankfurt am Main, FRG: Bernard and Graef, 1968,
pp. 434.

Cross-referenced by author, country and operation, a
comprehensive and useful source work in German for
materials in English and other Western languages up to
1968.   On the Russian and Soviet security and intelligence services and operations, see pp. 191-207 and
cross-references.

10. HAMMOND, Thomas Taylor, comp. and ed.

    SOVIET FOREIGN RELATIONS AND WORLD COMMUNISM;
    A SELECTED, ANNOTATED BIBLIOGRAPHY OF 7,000 BOOKS
    IN 30 LANGUAGES

    Princeton, New Jersey: Princeton University Press,
    1965, pp. 1240.

See pp. 1108-1119 for 109 selected items from the 1940s
to the 1960s on "Soviet Espionage", with perceptive
commentary by Robert M. Slusser. Especially useful is
the inventory of defector and official sources,
including U.S. Congressional publications.

11. HORACK, Stephen M., comp. and Rosemary
    NIESWENDER, ed.

    RUSSIA, THE USSR, AND EASTERN EUROPE:
    A BIBLIOGRAPHIC GUIDE TO ENGLISH LANGUAGE
    PUBLICATIONS, 1964-1974

    Littleton, Colorado: Libraries Unlimited, 1978,
    pp. 488.

See pp. 109-114 for selected annotated references to
Soviet "Police Terror, Propaganda, Espionage" from key
secondary works published in the 1960s and early
1970s.

12. HORECKY, Paul Louis, ed., Robert V. ALLEN and
    others, contributors

    RUSSIA AND THE SOVIET UNION: A BIBLIOGRAPHIC GUIDE
    TO WESTERN-LANGUAGE PUBLICATIONS

    Chicago, Illinois: University of Chicago Press,
    1965, pp. 473.

See pp. 172-180 for annotated, selected references to
Tsarist and Soviet "Police Powers" by Robert M.
Slusser. Comprises the principal titles in western
languages, but mostly in English, from the 1930s to the
1960s, dealing with "The Secret Police", "The Purges",
and "The System of Repression: Prisons, Concentration
Camps, Forced Labor."

13. JONES, David Lewis, comp.

   BOOKS IN ENGLISH ON THE SOVIET UNION, 1917-1973: A BIBLIOGRAPHY

   New York, New York: Garland, 1975, pp. 331.

An unannotated, general bibliography. For materials about Soviet security and intelligence activity see, "Political Institutions", pp. 81-85, "Political Process", pp. 89-93, and "Forced Labor", pp. 54-56.

14. LIBRARY OF CONGRESS, Congressional Research Service, **Soviet Intelligence and Security-Services**, Washington, D.C.: Government Printing Office, 1972-1975, Two volumes: I: **Soviet-Intelligence and Security Services, 1967-70: A Selected Bibliography of Soviet Publications**, with some additional titles from other sources, pp. 289. II: Covering 1971 and 1972, pp. 345 and 3 organizational charts.

A comprehensive, annotated survey of Soviet books, magazines, and press articles on intelligence, security and related material since the policy reversal of September 1964 regarding open media discussion of Soviet engagement in such activity.

15. PROKHOROV, Aleksandre Mikhailovich, ed.

   GREAT SOVIET ENCYCLOPEDIA

   [Bolshaya Sovietskaya Entsiklopedia]

   U.S. Edition: New York, New York: Macmillan, Third Edition, 1973-ongoing (31 volumes as of 1982).

   Russian Edition: Moscow, USSR: Third Edition, 1971-1978, 30 vols.

"A faithful translation of the Soviet national encyclopedia, unannotated and as true as possible to the concept and meaning intended by the editors..." Soviet limitations on writing and discussion about security and intelligence are evident in this primary source of Soviet popular knowledge, which is now available in English translation. Comparison of Western writings with the selected encyclopedic treatments cited below is an instructive exercise. See in the English edition:

"KGB", vol. 7, 685c; "State Security", vol. 7, 684d; "G.A.R. Aliyev", vol.1, 271b; "Iu.V. Andropov", vol. 2, 76b; "State Secrets", vol. 7, 684d; "F.E. Dzerzhinskiy", vol. 8, 476a, 482a, & vol. 14, 377b; "V.R. Menzhinskiy", vol. 16, 130d; "Cheka", vol. 5, 26d, & vol. 7, 68a; "Counterintelligence", vol. 13, 201c.

16. SCHATOFF, Michael, comp.

BIBLIOGRAFIIA OSVOBODITEL'NOGO DVIZHENIIA NARODOV ROSSII, 1941-1945

[Bibliography of the Russian People's Liberation Movement; 1941-1945]

New York, New York: All-Slavic Publishing House, 1961, pp. 208.

This bibliography has a direct bearing on Soviet intelligence. It identifies a number of books which deal with the KGB's attempt to disrupt or destroy the Vlasov movement.

17. SMITH, Edward E., with the collaboration of Rudolf LEDNICKY

THE OKHRANA - THE RUSSIAN DEPARTMENT OF POLICE, A BIBLIOGRAPHY

Stanford, California: Hoover Institution on War, Revolution and Peace, 1967, pp. 280.

Contains more than 800 items dealing with the Tsarist security service.

18. SMITH, Myron J. Jr.

THE SECRET WARS. A GUIDE TO SOURCES IN ENGLISH

Santa Barbara, California: ABC-Clio, 1980, 3 volumes.

Volume I: Intelligence, Propaganda and Psychological Warfare, Resistance Movements and Secret Operations, 1939-1945, introduction by Lyman B. Kirkpatrick, Jr. and chronology by Lloyd W. Garrison, pp. 312.

Volume II: <u>Intelligence, Propaganda and Psychol-</u>
<u>ogical Warfare, Covert Operations, 1945-1980,</u>
foreword by Harry Howe Ransom, pp. 471.

Volume III: <u>International Terrorism, 1968-1980,</u>
foreword and chronology by Lloyd W. Garrison, pp.
273.

A comprehensive and systematic, but unannotated general
intelligence bibliography. Specialized items dealing
with Soviet security and intelligence can be extracted
with careful attention to topical and personality cross
references. In Volume I see: "Secret Services...Soviet
Union", pp. 46-47, "Resistance...Soviet Union", pp.
144-149, and, "Propaganda & Psychological Warfare,
USSR", pp. 43-49. "Intelligence Espionage, and Covert
Operations around the World...USSR", pp. 182-188, and
"Some Personalities of the Secret Wars". Volume III
contains little about the USSR and terrorism.

19. U.S. CONGRESS, SENATE, Committee on Government
    Operations, **Congressional Investigations of Com-**
    munism and Subversive Activities. Summary-Index
    1918 to 1956, 84th Congress, 2nd Session, pp.
    382.

Some overlap with the Combined Cumulative Index
1951-1971 but stands on its own for the earlier period
1918-1950. Unique coverage of statements by the
illegals, Nicholas Dozenberg and Walter Krivitsky;
statements by Basil W. Delgass, Gregory B. Grafpen, and
others in the 1930 House investigations of the Soviet
use of Amtorg, New York and Michael Handler as intelligence cover.

20. U.S. CONGRESS, SENATE, **Subcommittee to Investigate**
    the Administration of the Internal Security Act
    and Other Internal Security Laws of the Committee
    on the Judiciary, 21 Year Index. Combined
    Cumulative Index, 1951-1971, 92nd Congress, 2nd
    Session.

Contains information on: Barmine, Bogolepov, Ege
(Akhemedov), Klimov (Kartkov), Rastvorov, Gouzenko,
Deriabin, Kaznacheyev, Alexander Orlov, Lawrence Britt
(Ladislav Bittman), Colonel Yevginey Y. Runge.

21. U.S. INFORMATION AGENCY, **Soviet Foreign Pro-**
paganda: An Annotated Bibliography, Washington,
D.C.: USIA Agency Library, FAR-15192, 1971, pp.
45.

This is an M.A. paper by Anne Boyer in partial ful-
fillment of a degree requirement at Catholic University.

22. UTECHIN, Sergei

A CONCISE ENCYCLOPEDIA OF RUSSIA

U.S. Edition: New York, New York: Dutton, 1964,
pp. 623.

U.K. Edition: Everyman's Concise Encyclopedia of
Russia, London, England: Dent, 1961, pp. 623.

Very brief but comprehensive entries. See: "Security
Organs", p. 478; "Cheka", p. 95; "GPU", p. 208; "KGB",
p. 265; "MGB", p. 350; "MVD", p. 366; "NKGB-NKVD", p.
300; "Leningrad Case", p. 316; "Beria", pp. 61-62;
"Dzerzhinskiy", p. 160; "Yagoda", p. 611; "Yezhov", p.
616; "Abakumov", p. 1; "Serov", p. 483; "Shelepin", p.
488; "Forced Labor", p. 186; "Smersh", p. 497.

23. VORE, Ronald M. de

SPIES AND ALL THAT...INTELLIGENCE AGENCIES AND
OPERATIONS: A BIBLIOGRAPHY

Los Angeles, California: Center for the Study of
Armament and Disarmament, California State University, 1977, pp. 71.

Political Issues Series, vol. 4, no. 3.

A general intelligence selection of 556 items, princi-
pally in English with brief annotations, of which about
a fifth are drawn from Soviet security and intelligence
materials of the last 40 years. Usefully cross-indexed
by subject.

24. WIECZYNSKI, Joseph L., ed.

THE MODERN ENCYCLOPEDIA OF RUSSIAN AND SOVIET HISTORY

Gulf Breeze, Florida: Academic International Press, 1976-ongoing, 34 volumes.

A comprehensive academic initiative with documented contributions. See entries for: "Cheka", vol. 6, pp. 190-218; "Katyn Forest Massacre", vol. 16, pp. 63-65; "KGB", vol. 7, pp. 197-203; "S.M. Kirov", vol. 17, pp. 33-37; "Commissariat of Internal Affairs", vol. 7, pp. 192-195; "GPU & OGPU", vol. 13, pp. 87-89; "Yan Karlovich Berzin", vol. 4, pp. 78-81; "L.P. Beria", vol. 4, 35-38; "N.I. Ezhov", vol. 5, pp. 34-39; "Labor Camps in the Soviet Union", vol. 18, pp. 236-242; et al.

25. ZORIN, Libushe

SOVIET PRISONS AND CONCENTRATION CAMPS: AN ANNOTATED BIBLIOGRAPHY 1917-1980

Newtonville, Massachusetts: Oriental Research Partners, 1980, pp. 118.

An indispensible tool for researching the history of the Soviet Gulag structure.

Section Two

Russian/Soviet Accounts

26.

CHEKISTY O SVOYEM TRUDE

[Chekists About Their Work]

Izvestiya Press, 1965, pp. 130.

English version available from the U.S. Department of Commerce, National Technical Information Service, Springfield, Va., Order No.: JPRS 55515, 23 March 1972, pp. 85.

Popularly written, factually guarded, anecdotal accounts and recollections by a selected group of security service operators.

27.

"V SESOYUSNOE SOVERSHCHANIYE"

[All Union Conference]

Izvestiya, 27 May 1981, p. 1.

28.

V TRADITSIYAKH SLAVNOGO FELIKSA

[In the Tradition of the Great Feliks]

Kommunist, No. 18, December 1977, pp. 59-68.

English version available from the Foreign Broadcast Information Service, 5003 CSO:1802, pp. 11.

In the Party's theoretical journal. Celebrates the 60th anniversary of the founding of the security service and the 100th anniversary of the birth of Dzerzhinskiy, its founder and first Chief.

29.

"MATERIALS ON THE 60TH ANNIVERSARY OF THE STATE SECURITY ORGANS"

<u>Translations on USSR Political & Sociological Affairs</u>, No. 842, pp. 22-47 (III-USSR-35).

English version available from the National Technical Information Service, Springfield, Va., Order No.: JPRS 70601, 7 February 1978.

Covers comments from nine of the Republics' KGB Chairmen and KGB Chiefs in Moscow and Leningrad. (Coverage is lacking on the 60th anniversary of the KGB in Armenian, Estonian, Lithuanian, Ukrainian and Uzbek SSRs.)

30.

"OBITUARY OF FILIP IVANOVICH GOLIKOV"

<u>Izvestiya</u>, <u>Pravda</u> and <u>Krasnaya Zvezda</u>, 1 August 1980.

This obituary for Filip Ivanovich Golikov (July 16, 1900-c. July 20, 1980. Chief of the GRU 1940-1941) was signed by Brezhnev, and by Party/Military leaders, but not by the present GRU Chief, Ivashutin.

31.

"SOVETSKIY ORGANY GOSUDARSTVENNOY BEZOPASTNOSTI V GODY VELIKOY OTECHESTVENNOY VOYNY"

[Soviet Organs of State Security in the Years of the Great Patriotic War]

<u>Voprosy Istoriy</u> (Questions of History), No. 5, May 1965, pp. 20-39.

This anonymous piece seems to have been part of the campaign to refurbish the State security service's

image that got under way in September 1964. It antici-
pated and preempted the impact of Aleksandre Nekrich's
critical study of the failure of Stalin and his
collaborators to anticipate the Nazi surprise attack on
June 22, 1941. Contains affirmations of "skillful
conduct" of deception by "organs of state security" in
1942 and 1943, but gives no supporting detail. Soviet
military intelligence resources are cited at a number
of points but credited to the security service.

32. ANDROPOV, Yuri

IZBRANNIYE RECHI I STAT'I

[Selected Speeches and Articles]

Moscow, USSR: Politizdat, 1979, pp. 318.

A fountainhead of "Andropoviana" meriting close study
and use. Includes a number of Andropov's speeches to
KGB cadres, published here for the first time. Properly
described by a Radio Liberty commentator as consti-
tuting "...the biggest boost in prestige the security
organs have received in the Soviet media since their
ideological demotion under Khrushchev...one of the
sharpest attacks on domestic dissent and its foreign
backers."

**"ANNOUNCING THE ISSUANCE OF ANDROPOV'S COLLECTED
SPEECHES AND ARTICLES"**

Pravda, 1 February 1980.

Only two predecessor chiefs of the Security Service,
Dzerzhinskiy and Beria, have been distinguished by
similar issuances.

33. ARDAMATSKIY, Vasiliy Ivanovich

VOZMEZDIYE

[Retribution]

Moscow, USSR: Molodaya Gvardiya, 1968, pp. 591.

Comprehensive account of the OGPU operation which lured
Boris Savinkov back into the country and the custody of
the security police in 1924. Useful because it makes
greater-than-usual textual use of case file materials.

34. BELIKOV, Il'ya Grigor'yevich with Ivan Kuz'mich
     BOIKO and Mikhail Semenovich LOGUNOV

     IMENI DZERZHINSKOGO

     [In the name of Dzerzhinskiy]

     Moscow, USSR: Voyenizdat, 1976, pp. 206.

A Soviet history of the special KGB/MVD Dzerzhinskiy
Division from its origins in the Civil War and the
1920s to the mid-1970s.

35. BELOV, G.A. et al., eds. and Aleksandre Kirikovich
     GONCHAROV comp.

     **IZ ISTORII VSEROSSIYSKOY CHREZVYCHAYNOY KOMISSII
     1917-1921gg. SBORNIK DOKUMENTOV**

     [From the History of the All-Russian Extraordinary
     Commission, 1917-1922. Documentary Collection]

     Moscow, USSR: Gosudarstvennoye Izdatel'stvo
     Politicheskoi Literaturi, 1958, pp. 487.

A highly selective documentary collection on the early
period of the Soviet security service. The principal
author was a security service officer and archives
specialist. Available in Russian from the Russian
Micro-Project, Dalhousie University (Killam Library,
Halifax, Nova Scotia B3H 4H8, Canada), among their
materials on the History of the state security apparatus.

36. CHEBRIKOV, V.M.

     "BDITEL'NOST' - ISPYTANNOYE ORUZHIE"

     [Vigilance - A Well-Tried Weapon]

     Molodoy Kommunist, No. 4, April 1981, pp. 28-34.

14

English version available from the Foreign
Broadcast Information Service 3 (June 1981): USSR
Annex, pp. 1-7.

For summary and commentary see, Elizabeth Teague, "KGB
Deputy Chief Warns of Western Propaganda Threat to
Soviet Youth", Radio Liberty Research RL 212/81 (May
22, 1981): pp. 4; and also a dispatch by Michael
Binyon, The Times (London), 14 May 1981, p. 9.

37.   CHISTYAKOV, N.F.

**"SOTSIALISTICHESKAYA ZAKONNOST' I SVAZ" S
SOVETSKOY OBSHCHESTVENNOST'YA—OSNOVNYYE PRINTSIPY
DEYATEL' NOSTI SLEDOVENNOGO APPARATA ORGANOV
GOSUDARSTVENNOY BEZOPASTNOSTI"**

[Socialist Law and Its Connection With the Soviet
Community - Basic Principles of the Activity of
the Investigative Apparatus of the State Security
Agencies.]

Sovietskoye Gosudarstvo I Pravo (Soviet State and
Law), No. 11, 1960, pp. 34-41.

Anecdotal piece by a retired KGB General based on
selected cases.

38.   DAVIS, Donald E. and Walter S.G. KOHN

"LENIN'S 'NOTEBOOK ON CLAUSEWITZ'"

Soviet Armed Forces Review Annual, vol. 1, edited
by David R. Jones.

Gulf Breeze, Florida: Academic International
Press, 1977, pp. 188-222.

A basic contribution. Translates and edits V.I. Lenin's
"Notebook of excerpts and remarks on Carl von Clausewitz: "'On War and the Conduct of War'" published in
the Leninskii Sbornik (Lenin Miscellany), 2nd edition,
Moscow/Leningrad, 1931, vol. 12, pp. 389-452.

39. DEMENTYEVA, Irina Aleksandrovna, Nikolay Ivanovich
AGAYANTS, and Yegor Vladimirovich YAKOVLEV

TOVARISHCH ZORGE

[Comrade Sorge]

Moscow, USSR: Sovetskaya Rossiya, 1965, pp. 134.

English version available from the U.S. Department
of Commerce, National Technical Information
Service, Springfield, Va., Order No.: JPRS 55492,
21 March 1972, pp. 54.

A widely-circulated human interest presentation of the
Sorge biography in the revisionist light of the
Sixties.

40. DULOV, A.V.

**OSNOVY PSIKHOLOGICHESKOGO ANALIZA NA PREVARITAL
NOM
SLEDSTVIY**

[Fundamentals of Psychological Analysis in Preliminary Investigation]

Moscow, USSR: Yuridicheskaya Literatura, 1973, pp.
168.

English version available from the U.S. Department
of Commerce, National Technical Information
Service, Springfield, Va., Order No., 61685, 8
April 1974, pp. 136.

From the annotative foreword: "This work is intended
for practicing personnel of investigative bodies of the
procurator's office, the MVD, and the KGB, for scientific personnel, and for students and instructors of
higher law schools." This piece, and others like it,
provide insight into contemporary security and security-
related techniques of interrogation and investigation.

41. DZERZHINSKIY, Felix Edmundovich

IZBRANNYE PROIZVEDENIYA

[Selected Works]

Moscow, USSR: Politizdat, 1967, Vol. 1: 1897-1923, pp. 590 & Vol. 2: 1924-July 1926, pp. 416.

A posthumous selection of Dzerzhinskiy's writings for the period 1897-1926, in lieu of an autobiography. A selective biographical chronology is included in Volume 1: pp. 560-578.

42. FOMIN, Fedor Timofeyevich

ZAPISKI STOROGO CHEKISTA

[Memoirs of an Old Chekist]

Moscow, USSR: Politizdat, 1st ed. 1962; 2nd ed. Moscow, USSR: corrected and supplemented, 1964, pp. 254.

English version available from the U.S. Department of Commerce, National Technical Information Service, Springfield, Va., Order No.: JPRS 55688, 12 April 1972, pp. 162.

Cheka memoirs which cover very selectively the period of the Revolution, the Civil War, the Twenties and the early Thirties. Fomin was the Chief or Deputy Chief of Military Counterintelligence (the Special Departments, or "OOs") of the 1st, 3rd, and 12th Red Armies in the Ukraine in 1919-1920; Chairman of the Crimean Cheka in 1921, and a leading official in the Leningrad Border Guards from the late 1920s until 1935. Extracts of the book first appeared in the magazine Neva in December 1957, and were among the first evidences of what has become a new, purposive genre of security and intelligence service writing in the Soviet Union since the early 1960s.

43. INAURI, A.N.

"EXCERPTS FROM SPEECH AT GEORGIAN IDEOLOGICAL SEMINAR"

Zarya Vostoka (Tiflis), 9 July 1981, pp. 3, 4.

On the same theme, see Elizabeth Fuller, "Transcaucasian KGB Chiefs Warn Against Ideological Subversion", Radio Liberty Research RL 5/81 (January 5,

1981): pp. 3. This summarizes and comments upon two articles by KGB Chiefs of Azerbaijan and Armenia, Major General Ziya Yusif-Zade and Major General Marius Yuzbashyan.

44. KASSIS, A.

"KIM PHILBY WITH A SAMOVAR"

Izvestiya, 4-10 August 1980.

An interview with Philby on the occasion of the first issuance in Russian of his memoir, My Silent War (q.v.), published in English in the United States in 1968.

45. KHENKIN, Kirill

L'ESPIONAGE SOVIETIQUE: LE CAS RUDOLF ABEL

[Soviet Espionage: The Case of Rudolph Abel]

French Edition: Paris, France: Fayard, 1981, pp. 371, traduite du russe par Alain Prechac.

Russian Edition: Okhotnik v Verkh Nogami (o Rudol'fe Abele i Villi Fishere (The Hunter Hunted, about Rudolph Abel and Willy Fisher). Frankfurt am Main, FRG: Posnev, 1980, pp. 312.

Khenkin is a Jewish intellectual, born in Russia, but raised in France after the Russian revolution. A volunteer partisan in Spain, he returned to the Soviet Union and is alleged to have had close association with Soviet state security, including access to William Fisher (Rudolph Abel), KGB illegal arrested by the FBI in New York in 1957.

46. KOLOSOV, Leonid Sergeiyevich and N. PETROV

"BESSMERTIYE PAVSHIKH"

[Immortality of Those Who Have Fallen]

Izvestiya; 8, 9, 10 October 1969, pp. 4, 6, and 4, respectively.

English version available from the U.S. Department
of Commerce, National Technical Information
Service, Springfield, Va., Order No.: JPRS 55490,
21 March 1972, pp. 34.

Describes the origins and the services rendered by a
Soviet World War II espionage net in Berlin (Schulze-
Boyson, Harnack, et al.) which German counterintelli-
gence called the Rote Kapelle or Red Orchestra.

47. KOZHEVNIKOV, Vadim Mikhaylovich

SHCHIT I MECH

[Shield and Sword]

Moscow, USSR: Izdatelstvo "Sovetskiy Pisatel",
1966, pp. 935.

English version available from the U.S. Department
of Commerce, National Technical Information
Service, Springfield, Va., Order No.: JPRS 56046-1
to 56046-4, 19 May 1972.

A fictionalized version of the agent career of Rudolf
Ivanovich Abel, who figures in this lengthy work by the
editor of the the prestigious Soviet journal Znamiya
(Banner) as Aleksandre Belov alias Johann Weiss (Abel=
A [leksandre] Bel [ov]). The pre-publication announce-
ment indicated that the book would consist of two
volumes. The first would describe Belov's life up to
the end of World War II; the second would deal with his
activity in the United States. This program was not
followed. Volume Two continued where Volume One had
ended treating Belov's activity against the Germans in
the Baltic and Eastern Poland. Closing abruptly with
the end of World War II and containing no information
about his life and activity in the United States or
elsewhere in the post-War period. Kozhevnikov's
treatment of Belov's recruitment, training, and
operational utilization by the Soviet state security
service in the 1920s and 1930s is totally at variance
with the known facts of Abel's origins and career. The
title refers to the KGB's logo.

48. MAL'KOV, Pavel Dmitriyevich

REMINISCENCES OF A KREMLIN COMMANDANT

translated from the Russian by V. Dutt

English Edition: Moscow, USSR: Progress Publishers, 1967, pp. 316.

Russian Edition: Zapiski Komendanta Moskovskogo Kremlya (Memoirs of a Kremlin Commandant), 1st ed. Moscow, USSR: 1961, pp. 285; 2nd ed. Moscow, USSR: Molodaya Gvardiya, 1967, pp. 263.

The Kremlin Guard is a primordial component of the Soviet Security Service. This piece, which first appeared in part in Moskva magazine (November 1958, pp. 123-161) covers the period from March 1918, immediately after the Cheka had moved its Headquarters from Petrograd to Moscow, to September 1919. On a number of points it is a documentary contribution. Mal'kov's account is "as told to" Andrey Yaklovyevich Yakovlev. "Yakovlev" was subsequently exposed in the samizdat publication, Political Diary, as the notorious Chekist, Andrei Yakovleyvich Sverdlov.

49. MATSULENKO, Viktor Antonovich

OPERATIVNAYA MASKIROVKA VOISK (PO OPYMU VELIKOY OTECHESTVENNOY VOYNY)

[Operational Military Camouflage and Deception. Based on the Experience of the Great Patriotic War]

Moscow, USSR: Voyenizdat, 1975, pp. 198.

Among the first of the book-length treatments in Russian of Soviet military camouflage and deception in World War II.

50. MATTHEWS, Mervyn, ed.

SOVIET GOVERNMENT. A SELECTION OF OFFICIAL DOCUMENTS ON INTERNAL POLICIES

New York, New York: Taplinger, 1974, pp. 472.

Pages 231-314 comprise translations of documents which
are related to the security service and its activity.
Among these is the full translation of the summary
protocol by the Council of Peoples' Commissars which
established the Cheka on 20 December 1917.

51. NIKULIN, Lev Ven'yaminovich.

THE DEADLY SWELL

Russian Editions: Mertvaya zyb'; Roman Khronika,
Moscow, USSR: Voyenizdat, 1965, pp. 359; Mertvaya
zyb'. Moscow, USSR: Sovetskiy Pisatel, 1966, pp.
590.

French Edition: La Houle; Nouvelle Historique
(trad. par Alexandre Karvoovski), Moscow, Editions
du Progres, 1969, pp. 384.

German Edition: Geheimakte Jakuschew (aus dem
Russischen ubersetzt v. Heinz Kubart), Berlin,
Germany: Deutscher Militarverl, 1969, pp. 269.
(NOTE: this is an abbreviated version of the
author's Tote Dunung.)

English translation of the original Russian
edition of this work under the title, The Swell of
the Sea, available from the U.S. Department of
Commerce, National Technical Information Service,
Springfield, Va., Order No.: JPRS 55686, 1972, pp.
237.

The Trust ("Trest") Operation, 1921-1927, is retold
with significant changes in fact and emphasis from
versions propagated in the Twenties, and sponsored by
the Soviets after World War II in the work published by
Michael Sayers and Albert E. Kahn, The Great Conspiracy. The Secret War Against the Soviet Union
(q.v.).

52. OSTRYAKOV, Sergei Zakharovich

VOYENNYE CHEKISTY

[Military Chekists]

Moscow, USSR: Voyenizdat, 1979, pp. 320.

A selective but useful account of the KGB's Third Chief
Directorate (Armed Forces Counterintelligence and Security) and its predecessors, including SMERSH.

53.   PANKRATOV, L.I.

    "AN INTERVIEW WITH L.I. PANKRATOV"

    <u>Trud</u>, 19 December 1967, pp. 1-3.

    English version available from the Foreign
    Broadcast Information Service, USSR, 10 January
    1968.

This interview with the Deputy Chairman of the KGB was
timed for the 50th anniversary of the founding of the
security service. In the course of the interview Pankratov continued the effort to accredit the
belief that the security service had been successful in
securing advance warning of the impending German attack
in the period April-June 1941.

54.   RINALDI, Giorgio

    TAINIK (NASCONDIGLIO)

    [Dead Drop-Secret Hiding Place]

    Legnano, Italy: Landon, 1976, pp. 340.

In Italian, these are post-imprisonment memoirs by an
unrepentant agent of the GRU.

55.   SAPAROV, Arif Vasil'yevich

    BITAYA KARTA. KHRONIKA ODINOGO ZAGOVORA

    [The Game is Up. Chronicle of a Conspiracy]

    Leningrad, USSR: Lenizdat, 1967, pp. 213.

    English version available from the U.S. Department
    of Commerce, National Technical Information
    Service, Springfield, Va., Order No.: JPRS 55467,
    17 March 1972, pp. 215.

The Soviets recount the case of British intelligence
operative Paul Dukes, "ST-25", and the liquidation of
the anti-Soviet organization known as "The National
Center."

56.   SHIMANSKY, A.

"O DOSTIZHENIY STRATEGICHESKIY VNEZAPNOSTI PRI PODGOTOVKE LETNE-OSENNEY KAMPANIY 1944 GODA"

[Concerning the Achievement of Strategic Surprise in the Preparation for the Summer-Fall Campaign of 1944]

Voyenno Istorichesky Zhurnal (Journal of Military History), No. 6, 1968, pp. 17-28.

See Soviet Military Translations No. 467, "1944 Summer-Fall Campaign on the Eastern Front."

One of the first Soviet studies of their own operations in "strategic camouflage and deception" in World War II.

57.   SLOCHANYK, Roman

"UKRAINIAN KGB CHIEF WARNS OF IDEOLOGICAL SABOTAGE"

Radio Liberty Research RL 422/81 (October 22, 1981): pp. 4.

A detailed review of two articles in Ukrainian CP publications during 1981 on the alleged rising threat of western ideological sabotage against the Soviet Union and Socialist countries, particularly Poland.

58.   SOFINOV, P.G.

OCHERKI ISTORII VSEROSSIYSKOY CHREZVYCHAYNOY KOMISSII 1917-1921gg

[Historical Notes on the All-Russian Extra-ordinary Commission]

Moscow, USSR: Gospolitizdat, 1960, pp. 247.

A slanted narrative-interpretive rendition of the documentary materials in the Belov publication. Available in Russian from the Russian Micro Project. See entry #35 for address.

59.   STRUVE, Gleb, ed.

"NOVOYE O TRESTE"

[New Materials About 'Trust']

Noviy Zhurnal, No. 125, 1976, pp. 194-214.

This article is testimony to the continuing impact of
the Trust political deception operation on the Russian
emigration.

60.   TEVEKELYNA, Vartkes Arutyunovich

REKLAMNOYE BYURO GOSPODINA KOCHEKA

[Mr. Kochek's Advertising Agency]

Moscow, USSR: Sovetskiy Pisatel, 1970, pp. 415.

English version available from the U.S. Department
of Commerce, National Technical Information
Service, Springfield, Va., Order No.: JPRS 55530,
24 March 1972, pp. 340.

A contrived, synthetic account of the activity of a
husband-wife illegal team operating in France, Germany,
Switzerland and the United States in the 1930s and
1940s. It incorporates elements of at least three
real-life models.

61.   TISHKOV, Arseny Vasilyevich

FELIX DZERZHINSKIY. COMMEMORATING THE CENTENARY OF
HIS BIRTH

Moscow, USSR: Novosti Publishing House, 1977, pp.
76.

A summary in English of a highly colored biography of
Dzerzhinskiy, first published by Tishkov in 1968 under
the title, Perviy Chekist (The First Chekist). Tishkov
is a former senior officer of the security service.

62. TSINEV, G.

"SAMOYE OSTROYE ORUZHIYE"

[The Sharpest Weapon]

Znamenosets (Standard Bearer), June 1980.

The author credits the Party with the victory over Germany in World War II. Tsinev himself is not credited as a KGB Deputy Chairman.

63. TSVIGUN, Semun Kuz'mich.

"PODRIVNIYE AKTSII-ORUZHIYE IMPERIALISMA"

[Subversive Acts - Imperialism's Weapon]

Kommunist, No. 4, March 1980, pp. 109-119.

"O PROISKAKH IMPERIALISTICHESKIKH RAZVEDOK"

[Regarding the Intrigues of Imperialistic Intelligence Agencies]

Kommunist (Moscow), No. 14, September 1981, pp. 88-99.

English version available from the Foreign Broadcast Information Service, 16 October 1981, Annex, pp. 1-10. Also Serge Schmemann, "Dissidents Routed KGB Chief Says...," New York Times, 7 October 1981.

Tsvigun, asserted to be Brezhnev's brother-in-law, was First Deputy Chairman, KGB from December 1967 until his death in January 1982. He was a principal in the written and other media projection of the enhanced KGB image.

64. TSVIGUN, Semun Kuz'mich, et al., eds.

FELIKS EDMUNDOVICH DZERZHINSKIY: BIOGRAFIYA

[Feliks Edmundovich Dzerzhinskiy: A Biography]

Moscow, USSR: Politizdat, 1977, pp. 494.

Biographical collection of writings on the Cheka's founder by the late First Deputy KGB Chairman. A "Second and Enlarged Edition" was issued in 1983. Although identical in the total number of pages, all references and content attributable to Tsvigun are dropped.

65. TSYBOV, Sergey Ivanovich and Nikolay Fedorovich CHISTYAKOV

FRONT TAYNOY VOYNY

[Front of the Secret War]

Moscow, USSR: 1st edition: Voyenizdat, 1965, pp. 158. 2nd edition: Voyenizdat, 1968, pp. 205.

English version available from the U.S. Department of Commerce, National Technical Information Service, Springfield, Va., Order No.: AD 714 739, 1971, pp. 166.

The Soviets present the official review of the protean effort of the security service to safeguard the USSR from its foreign enemies, beginning with the case of the "National Center" and Bruce Lockhart in 1918, and ending with the ideological subversion by the Jehovah's Witnesses in the mid-Sixties. Chistyakov was a senior security service legal officer. This book is unusual for its treatment of both the Popov and the Penkovskiy cases.

66. VASIL'YEV, Arkadiy

"V CHAS DNYA, VASHE PREVOSKHODITEL'STVO..."

[At One O'clock In The Afternoon, Your Excellency...]

Moscow, USSR: Khudyzh-literatura, 1975, pp. 425.

English version available from the National Technical Information Service, Springfield, Va., Order No.: JPRS 56096-1 and 56096-2, 25 May 1972, pp. 519.

A fictionalized narrative, allegedly based on facts, about the penetration of the headquarters of the Russian Liberation Army (ROA) commanded by the Soviet defector to the Germans, General Andrey Andreyevich Vlasov, by two Soviet security officers. It was also published as a serial in the Moscow magazine Moskva in: No. 8, August 1967, pp. 10-30; No. 9, September 1967, pp. 6-133; No. 8, August 1969, pp. 8-60; No. 9, September 1969, pp. 55-165.

67.   VASSILIEV, A.T.

THE OKHRANA, THE RUSSIAN SECRET POLICE

London, England: G.G. Harrap, 1930, pp. 319.

A favorable and factual account of the Tsarist security service by its last chief.

68.   VOSTOKOV, Vladimir and Oleg SHMELEV

"POSLEDNYAYA OSHIBKA REZIDENTA"

[The Resident Agent's Last Mistake]

Ogonek, No. 38 through 49, 1965, pp. 20-23; 10-13; 18-21; 20-24; 10-13; 18-21; 17-21; 18-21; 18-21; 17-21; 12-15; 18-22 respectively.

English version available from the U.S. Department of Commerce National Technical Information Service, Springfield, Va., Order No.: JPRS 55597, 31 March 1972, pp. 218.

A model case from the KGB standpoint: a Western intelligence agent is identified and eventually arrested in the USSR; his Western sponsor is controlled through one of his "recruits" who was in actuality a skillful officer-operative of the Soviet security service. A novel, it was republished in a second edition under the title Oshibka Rezidenta (The Resident's Mistake). Moscow, USSR: Molodaya Gvardiya, 1974, pp. 350.

69. YUDIN, N.F.

PERVAYA PARTIZANSKAYA

[The First Partisan Division]

Moscow, USSR: Izdatel'stvo Moskovskiy Rabochiy, 1983, pp. 352.

Popularly-written account of the Smolensk Partisan Division which operated behind German lines 1941-1943. Useful for probing the roots of contemporary SPETSNAZ formations subordinate to military intelligence and state security.

70. ZUBOV, Nikolay Ivanovich

F.E. DZERZHINSKIY: BIOGRAFIYA

[F.E. Dzerzhinskiy. Biography]

Moscow, USSR: 1st edition: Politizdat, 1963, pp. 334; 2nd edition: Politizdat, 1965, pp. 364; 3rd edition: Politizdat, 1971, pp. 423.

Issued in 1963, this panegyric to the security service's founder was materially corrected and embellished in 1965. Additional changes were made in the 1971 revision.

Section Three

Defector/First Hand Accounts

Books

71. AGABEKOV, George

OPGU: THE RUSSIAN SECRET TERROR

1st American edition, translated from the French by Henry W. Bunn. New York, New York: Brentano's 1931, pp. 277.

2nd edition. Westport, Connecticut: Hyperion Press, 1975, pp. 277.

Above are English translations from the French of the 1st Russian edition of Agabekov's memoirs, G.P.U. (Zapiski Chekista) [The G.P.U. (Memoirs of a Chekist)]. Berlin, Germany: Izdatel'stvo "Strela", 1930, pp. 247.

An Italian translation published in 1932: La GPU. Memorie di un membro della Ceca. Milan, Italy: Treves, 1932, pp. 312.

A second memoir appeared in Russian in 1931, Ch.Ka Za Rabotoy [The Cheka at Work] Berlin, Germany: Izdatel'stvo "Strela", 1931, pp. 334.

There was a Spanish language translation of this book, Stalin en el Oriente medio, translated from the Russian by Maurico Carlavilla ["Mauricio Karl"]. Madrid, Spain: Graficas Valera, 1946, pp. 317.

A composite edition drawn selectively from Agabekov's Russian writings was, Die Tscheka bei der Arbeit, translated by A. Chanock. Stuttgart, Germany: Union Deutsche Verlagsgesellschaft, 1935, pp. 207.

Agabekov worked for the Cheka and the GPU from 1920 to 1930, when he defected in Istanbul and made his way to Paris. His principal assignments were in Turkestan, Iran, Afghanistan and Turkey.

Immediately after his defection, he published a series of articles in the Paris emigre organ, Posledniye Novosti [Latest News]. A translation of a reprint by the Novoye Russkoye Slovo (New York City), 13 October 1930, "O.G.P.U.--Reminiscences of the Chekist, G. Agabekoff," appears in the Hearings before a Special Committee to Investigate Communist Activities in the United States. House of Representatives. Seventy-First Congress, Second Session. Part I--Volume No. 5, December 1930, pp. 147-54.

Agabekov's detailed information on Soviet operations among the Armenians was embodied in a series of ten articles (of which, apparently, only nine were published) in the Armenian emigre publication in Cairo, Egypt, Husaber, c. October 1931. Agabekov disappeared in Brussels in 1938, presumably a victim of Soviet assassination.

These and other writings by Agabekov are fundamental to an understanding of Soviet security and intelligence organization and operations in the 1920s, especially in the Near and Middle East.

72. AKHMEDOV, Ismail (Ismail Ege)

IN AND OUT OF STALIN'S GRU: A TATAR'S ESCAPE FROM RED ARMY INTELLIGENCE

Frederick, Maryland: University Publications of America, Inc., 1984, pp. 222

By the first Soviet serving military intelligence defector to the West [1942]. Eyewitness details regarding the Soviet failure to perceive the German surprise attack in June 1941 notwithstanding the intelligence warning. An important memoir which amplifies his Congressional testimony (entry #482).

73. ALLILUEVA, Svetlana

ONLY ONE YEAR

translated from the Russian Tol'ko Odin God by Paul Chavchavadze

U.S. Edition: New York, New York: Harper & Row,
1969, pp. 444.

U.K. Edition: London, England: Hutchinson, 1969,
pp. 415.

A moving and evocative presentation of the spirit of
the Soviet regime, including comments on Security
Service personalities by Stalin's daughter, who
returned to the Soviet Union with her 13 year old
American daughter in November 1984.

74. AMALRIK, Andrei

NOTES OF A REVOLUTIONARY

translated by Guy Daniels from the Russian Zapiski
Dissidenta with an introduction by Susan Jacoby

New York, New York: Knopf, 1982, pp. 343.

Published posthumously following Amalrik's untimely
death in Spain in 1980. Covers the last ten years in
the USSR before his exile in 1976 to the West. Coverage
includes the world of informers and double agents
(among the Soviet populace) and KGB efforts to recruit
Amalrik right up to his departure from the USSR.

75. ANTONOV–OVSEYENKO, Anton

THE TIME OF STALIN: PORTRAIT OF A TYRANNY

translated from the Russian Portret Tirana by
George Saunders with an introduction by Stephen F.
Cohen

New York, New York: Harper & Row, 1981, pp. 374.

A superb memoir and expose of Stalin's despotism by the
son of V.A. Antonov-Ovseyenko--old Bolshevik and
one-time chief Army Commissar, State Prosecutor and
diplomat who was executed in the late 1930s. Some
consider this work to be on the qualitative level of
Solzhenitsyn's Gulag and Medvedev's Let History Judge.

76. AVTORKHANOV, Abdurakhman

THE COMMUNIST PARTY APPARATUS

Chicago, Illinois: Henry Regnery, 1966, pp. 422.

Avtorkhanov is one of the leading exponents of the
theory of Party domination of the Security Service. See
especially Chapter XVII, "Party Direction of the Soviet
Police."

77. BARMINE, Alexandre

**MEMOIRS OF A SOVIET DIPLOMAT: TWENTY YEARS IN THE
SERVICE OF THE USSR**

translated by Gerard Hopkins

London, England: L. Dickson, 1938, pp. 360.

A teenager at the time of the Revolution, the author
later occupied several positions in the Soviet government: military, industrial, and lastly diplomatic. He
defected, fled to France, then to the US in reaction to
the horror of the purges and trials in the USSR.
Barmine served in France, Italy, Belgium, Poland, and
Greece, and his works describe Soviet intelligence
operations there.

78. --------

**ONE WHO SURVIVED: THE LIFE STORY OF A RUSSIAN
UNDER THE SOVIETS**

introduction by Max Eastman

New York, New York: Putnam, 1945, pp. 337.

This book deals with information on undercover na-
tionals, social conditions, and economic disorgani-
zation in the USSR. The stress is on the pre-1937
period in Soviet history.

79. BESSEDOVSKY, Grigory

REVELATIONS OF A SOVIET DIPLOMAT

translated and abridged from the Russian <u>Na Putiakh K Termidoru</u> by Matthew Norgate

U.S. Edition: Westport, Connecticut: Hyperion Press, 1977, pp. 276 (reprint of 1931 U.K. edition).

U.K. Edition: London, England: Williams and Norgate, 1931, pp. 276 (abridged translation of <u>Na Putiakh K Termidoru</u>).

French Edition: <u>Oui J'Accuse! Au Service des Soviets</u>, Paris, France: Libraire de La Revue Francaise, A. Redier, 1930, pp. 265.

German Edition: <u>Den Klaven Der Tscheka Entronnen : Erinnerungen.</u> Deutsch von N. von Gersdorff, Leipzig, Germany, Grethlein & Co., 1930, pp. 343.

Bessedovsky, a diplomat, defected from the Soviet embassy in Paris in October 1929. He is one of the controversial defectors whose various literary ventures spurred charges by some observers ranging from fabrication for profit to outright disinformation on Moscow's behalf. The above account is one of several versions, all troublesome, dealing with his official experiences and the circumstances of his defection. See Brook-Shepherd, <u>The Storm Petrels</u> (q.v.), for another account of Bessedovsky's odyssey and enterprises.

80. BITTMAN, Ladislav

THE DECEPTION GAME: CZECHOSLOVAK INTELLIGENCE IN SOVIET POLITICAL WARFARE

Syracuse, New York: Syracuse University Research Corp., 1972, pp. 246.

Reissued by Ballantine Books, New York, New York: 1981, pp. 244.

This thought-provoking book provides an "insider's" view into deception and disinformation operations as practiced by the Soviet and Czech intelligence services. It is the work of a former Czech intelligence officer whose service included that of Deputy Chief of

Department D from 1964 through 1966. Bittman defected in 1968. His book is one of the best available sources on Soviet/Bloc deception operations.

81. BORODIN, Nikolai M.

ONE MAN IN HIS TIME

U.S. Edition: New York, New York: Macmillan, 1955, pp. 343.

U.K. Edition: London, England: Constable, 1955, pp. 343.

A Soviet biologist describes his life and the political restrictions and police intervention in science in the USSR. The author cooperated with the CHEKA, and became scientific consultant to the NKVD. He illuminates intensified Soviet efforts at industrial espionage in the postwar period.

82. BOURKE, Sean

THE SPRINGING OF GEORGE BLAKE

U.S. Edition: New York, New York: Viking Press, 1970, pp. 364.

U.K. Edition: London, England: Cassell, 1970, pp. 355.

An interesting account of the escape of convicted British intelligence officer, George Blake, a Soviet penetration agent. Written by the Irishman who helped engineer the operation, the book describes the escape plot, the personality of Blake, and the operations of the KGB in the Soviet Union after Blake and Bourke were re-united in Moscow. Bourke subsequently returned to Ireland and is recently deceased.

83. CHAMBERS, Whittaker

WITNESS

U.S. Edition: New York, New York: Random House, 1952, pp. 808.

34

U.K. Edition: London, England: A. Deutsch, 1953, pp. 629.

An important and still controversial memoir by a former principal in major Soviet political and intelligence (GRU) operations in the US from the 1920s to the late 1930s. See Weinstein's, Perjury: The Hiss-Chambers Case (q.v.) for an objective study of the controversy.

84. DERIABIN, Peter

WATCHDOGS OF TERROR: RUSSIAN BODYGUARDS FROM THE TSARS TO THE COMMISSARS

New Rochelle, New York: Arlington House, 1972, pp. 448.

Revised and enlarged edition: Frederick, Maryland: University Publications of America, Inc., 1984, pp. 456.

Drawing on personal experiences and numerous Russian and Western sources, Deriabin traces the history of internal security from Kievan Russia to the Soviet Union of the 1980s. Deriabin shows how the bodyguard system within the KGB's Ninth Directorate and its predecessors have been used as an instrument of terror against both the general populace and the Party apparatus itself. Providing insights into the structure and workings of the various echelons of the Security Services, Deriabin also presents credible accounts of incidents discussed nowhere else: assassination attempts against Stalin; details of the arrest of Beria and his lieutenants; and KGB insubordination during Khrushchev's reign, among others. A substantial appendix gives details on such items as "Okhrana" organization, pay scales, training, and the Kremlin Kommandatura. The revised edition continues the narrative through the post-Brezhnev succession.

85. DERIABIN, Peter and Frank GIBNEY

THE SECRET WORLD

U.S. Edition: Garden City, New York: Doubleday, 1959, pp. 334.

French Edition: Deriabine, Pierre et Frank Gibney, traduit de l'americain par Pierre Copin, Policier de Staline, Paris, France: Fayard, 1966, pp. 275.

Reissued by Ballantine Books, New York, New York, 1982 with a new introduction and an updated review of personalities, pp. 405.

This memoir is one of the best available expositions on KGB operations, organization, and missions. The author was a KGB Major in the intelligence directorate when he defected from his post in Vienna in February, 1954. The Secret World is the KGB's organizational biography as known to the author during his ten years of service in Soviet State Security.

86. DNEPROVETS, A. [pseudonym]

YEZHOVSHCHINA: ZABYT' NEL'ZYA...

[Yezhovshchina: It is Impossible to Forget]

Munich, FRG: Izdanie Tsentral'nogo Ob'yedineniya Politicheskikh Emigrantov iz SSSR [Tsope], 1958, pp. 55.

Pseudonymous account, with considerable detail on the Yezhov purge period in the late 1930s in Dnepropetrovsk oblast and city. The listing of one Chernenko (p. 42)--no first name or middle initial--as a member of the Dnepropetrovsk NKVD at that time, has contributed to serious speculation that the recently deceased CPSU General Secretary was an NKVD participant in the purges.

87. DYADKIN, Iosif G.

UNNATURAL DEATHS IN THE USSR 1928-1954

translated by Tania Deruguine

New Brunswick, New Jersey: Transaction Books, 1983, pp. 63.

Dyadkin was a professor of geophysics before his arrest in 1980 for writing this work and sending it to Alexandr Solzhenitsyn. His research concludes that a combination of Soviet state terror and World War II claimed between 43 and 52 million Soviet lives from

1928-1954. During the last three years of Stalin's rule alone (1950-1953) 450,000 died in the camps, according to Dyadkin's calculations.

88. FOOTE, Alexandre

HANDBOOK FOR SPIES

U.S. Edition: Garden City, New York: Doubleday, 1949, pp. 273.

U.K. Edition: London, England: Museum Press, 1964, pp. 192 (revised edition).

The RAND Corporation published initial commments, printed in 1949 as research memo RM-207a.

Description of the Soviet GRU espionage net, "Rote Drei", in Switzerland during World War II, written by its British radio operator. Also, see and compare Ruth Werner (q.v.).

89. FROLIK, Josef

THE FROLIK DEFECTION

London, England: Leo Cooper, 1975, pp. 184.

These memoirs of a Czech intelligence officer who defected in 1969, are a good guide to the day-to-day operations of Bloc intelligence operatives. Frolik details poisoning and bombing attempts against Radio Free Europe, entrapment of visitors to his country, recruitment of members of the British Parliament, and cultivation of certain British labor leaders.

90. GOLITSYN, Anatoliy

NEW LIES FOR OLD: COMMUNIST STRATEGY OF DECEPTION AND DISINFORMATION

New York, New York: Dodd Mead, 1984, pp. 592.

Golitsyn's first public word since defecting to the West in 1961 and an extremely important, albeit in certain aspects controversial, contribution to the

literature. Includes the first detailed account of:
Shelepin's 1959 KGB reorientation and reorganization;
the May 1959 conference of senior KGB, Party and State
officials; and the creation of Department D (disinformation) under the tutelage of Colonel Agayants.

91. GOUZENKO, Igor

THE IRON CURTAIN

Written partly in English and partly in Russian
and rewritten by A.W. O'Brien

U.S. Edition: New York, New York: E.P. Dutton,
1948, pp. 279.

Canadian Edition: This Was My Choice, Montreal,
Canada: Palm Publishing, 1968 [c1948], pp. 238
(2nd edition).

The author's defection on September 5, 1945, in Ottawa,
where he was the Soviet Military Intelligence (GRU)
code clerk, launched the still continuing, world-wide
awareness of the scope and depth of the Soviet intelligence threat. (See the Canadian Royal Commission Report
which validated and accredited his testimony and extensive documentary evidence.)

In this book Gouzenko tells his own life story and
reviews GRU and NKVD (State Security) organization and
operational activity within the USSR and abroad during
the 1935-1945 period, including operations targeted
against Canadian and American atomic projects.

92. GRANOVSKIIY, Anatoliy

**I WAS AN NKVD AGENT: A TOP SOVIET SPY TELLS HIS
STORY**

New York, New York: Devin-Adair Company, 1962, pp.
343.

In 1942 the author was admitted to the special school
of the NKVD for the training of partisan personnel.
After the war he was assigned to Czechoslovakia.
Recalled from Prague when he attempted to save his
principal agent, he was next assigned to security work
in the Soviet Merchant Navy. He left his ship in the

fall of 1946 in Stockholm and was granted Swedish asylum. He was among the first post World War II defectors from the Soviet Security Service.

93. GRIGORENKO, Petr Grigorevich

MEMOIRS

New York, New York: Norton, 1982, pp. 462.

Important, insightful testimony about how and why Stalin retained party mass support in the Twenties and Thirties, and to the KGB's adaptive methodology in the handling of dissent in the Sixties and Seventies.

Chapter X, "Intelligence Summary Number Eight" (pp. 114-121) is a unique contribution to the understanding of the failure of Stalin and the General Staff to anticipate the German surprise attack on June 21, 1941.

94. ---------

THE GRIGORENKO PAPERS

with an introduction by Edward Crankshaw

Boulder, Colorado: Westview Press, 1976, pp. 187.

See Chapter I on the failure of Stalin and the Soviet Armed Forces to anticipate the German surprise attack in 1941 (pp. 7-51). This presentation supplements the facts and interpretation developed by A.M. Nekrich in his 1965 monograph. See also, Chapter V, "The Power of the KGB", which is concerned with the KGB's handling of Grigorenko's own case (pp. 75-125).

95. HUMINIK, John

DOUBLE AGENT

New York, New York: The New American Library, 1967, pp. 181.

A description of six years spent fencing with the KGB in Washington and New York under FBI control.

96. IVANOV-RAZUMNIK, R.V. [Razmunik Valilevich Ivanov]

THE MEMOIRS OF IVANOV-RAZUMNIK

translated and annotated from the Russian <u>Tiur'my</u>
<u>I Ssylki</u> by P.S. Squire, with an introduction by
G. Jankovsky

London, England: Oxford University Press, 1965,
pp. 374.

An important memoir on the Security Service's operational role in the period of the "Great Terror". The
author died in the West in 1946.

97. JOHN, Otto

**TWICE THROUGH THE LINES: THE AUTOBIOGRAPHY OF OTTO
JOHN**

translated from the German <u>Zweimal Kam Ich Heim</u> by
Richard Barry, with an introduction by H.R.
Trevor-Roper

U.S. Edition: New York, New York: Harper & Row,
1972, pp. 340.

U.K. Edition: London, England: Macmillan, 1972,
pp. 340.

These memoirs of the former head of West Germany's
post-World War II internal Security Service are his
account of his "defection" or "kidnapping" to East
Germany and his subsequent return to West Germany.
John's story has been confirmed by reliable defectors
from the Soviet Security Service.

98. KAMINSKAYA, Dina

**FINAL JUDGEMENT: MY LIFE AS A SOVIET DEFENSE
ATTORNEY**

translated by Michael Glenny

New York, New York: Simon & Schuster, 1982, pp.
364.

One of the best informed pieces extant on the workings
and vagaries of the Soviet judicial system. Especially

useful for the role of State Security in the judicial process.

99.   KAZNACHEYEV, Alexandre

INSIDE A SOVIET EMBASSY: EXPERIENCES OF A RUSSIAN DIPLOMAT IN BURMA

edited, with an introduction by Simon Wolin

Philadelphia, Pennsylvania: Lippincott, 1962, pp. 250.

In 1957 the author was assigned to the Soviet embassy in Burma as a translator-interpreter. There he was transferred (i.e."co-opted") from the diplomatic corps to the KGB for local political influence and infiltration work. His book provides insight into Soviet combined diplomatic and political activity in Southeast Asia under embassy cover. Kaznacheyev's case is an early example of co-optation for "active measures" in the field.

100. KHODOROVICH, Tatayana Sergeevna

THE CASE OF LEONID PLYUSHCH

translated by Marite Sapiers, Peter Redaway, and Caryl Emerson

Boulder, Colorado: Westview Press, 1976, pp. 152.

This work deals vividly with Ukrainian political dissidents and the weapons employed by the Soviet government to curtail them. The use of psychiatric hospitals is well-documented.

101. KHOKHLOV, Nikolai Y.

IN THE NAME OF CONSCIENCE

translated by Emily Kingsbury

U.S. Edition: New York, New York: David McKay Co., 1959, pp. 365.

U.K. Edition: London, England: F. Muller, 1960, pp. 356.

German Report: <u>Ich Sollte Morden; ein Tatsachen-</u>
<u>bericht</u>, Frankfurt am Main, FRG: F. Rudl, 1954,
pp. 45.

Russian Edition: <u>Pravno na Sovest</u>, Frankfurt am
Main, FRG: 1957, pp. 612.

A frank and revelatory autobiographical account of the
experiences of a State Security "executive action"
officer from his recruitment in 1941 to his defection
in 1954. In that year, Khokhlov was sent to Germany to
assassinate a prominent leader of the NTS (an anti-
Soviet Russian emigre organization). Refusing to carry
out this execution, he defected to US intelligence
officials. Khokhlov himself was then the target of a
nearly successful assassination attempt by the KGB's
"Wet Affairs" department.

102. KOPELEV, Lev

EASE MY SORROWS: A MEMOIR

translated by Antonina W. Bovis

New York, New York: Random House, 1983, pp. 256.

Third volume in a continuing series of memoirs of a
former political prisoner. This volume relates the
author's detention and work in a Moscow prison-
laboratory, a "Sarashka", with, among others, Alexandr
Solzhenitsyn.

103. KRASNOV, N.N., Jr.

THE HIDDEN RUSSIA: MY TEN YEARS AS A
SLAVE LABORER

[Nezabivaimoye, 1945-1956]

New York, New York: Holt, Rinehart & Winston,
1960, pp. 351.

See pp. 190-194 for author's interview in the Lubyanka
Prison, Moscow, after forcible return from Austria by
the NKGB chief, Vsevolod Merkulov. On the author's
death at age 49 in Buenos Aires, attributed to poisoning by the Soviets, see Nikolai Tolstoy, <u>The Secret</u>
<u>Betrayal</u> (U.K. Edition: <u>Victims of Yalta</u>) (q.v.).

104. KRIVITSKY, Walter G. [Samuel Ginzburg]

IN STALIN'S SECRET SERVICE: AN EXPOSE OF RUSSIA'S SECRET POLICIES BY THE FORMER CHIEF OF SOVIET INTELLIGENCE IN WESTERN EUROPE

Westport, Connecticut: Hyperion Press, 1979, pp. 273.

Reprint of the 1939 edition: New York, New York: Harper and Brothers, 1939.

A basic work of defector literature. Krivitsky served in Soviet military intelligence (GRU) from 1920 to the early thirties when he transferred to State Security. From 1933/34-1937, when he defected in Paris, he was a NKVD illegal resident in the Hague. Along with a number of others like Agabekov, Orlov, and Barmine, he is one of the important defectors of that era. His death in Washington, D.C. in 1941, though officially labeled a suicide, is still suspected to be a Soviet assassination.

105. KUUSINEN, Aino

THE RINGS OF DESTINY: INSIDE SOVIET RUSSIA FROM LENIN TO BREZHNEV

translated from the German Der Gott Storzt Seine Engel by Paul Stevenson with a foreword by Wolfgang Leonhard and a preface by John H. Hodgson

New York, New York: Morrow, 1974, pp. 255.

A personal account by the widow of the late Comintern and Soviet Party luminary, Otto Kuusinen. Valuable for the insights given to the Shanghai phase, in the 1930's, of the intelligence activities of the GRU operative, Richard Sorge, and his colleagues in China and Japan. Provides information and leads not available in other accounts of Sorge's operations (eg. Deakin & Storry, The Case of Richard Sorge [q.v.]).

106. KUZNETSOV, Edward

PRISON DIARIES

translated from the Russian Dnevniki by Howard Spier, with an introduction by Leonard Schapiro

U.S. Edition: New York, New York: Stein & Day, 1975, pp. 254.

U.K. Edition: London, England: Vallentine, Mitchell, 1975, pp. 256.

A vivid contemporary insight into KGB modus operandi and the prison regimes in Leningrad, Moscow and elsewhere. The author was the principal defendant in the 1970 abortive attempt to hijack a plane from Leningrad.

107. LOCKHART, Robert Hamilton Bruce

BRITISH AGENT

with an introduction by Hugh Walpole

1st U.S. Edition: New York, New York: G.P. Putnam's Sons, 1933, pp. 354.

2nd U.S. Edition: Garden City, New York: Garden City Publishing Co., 1936, pp. 254.

A memoir by a British representative entrapped through a Cheka provocation in 1918. After a month in Cheka custody he was exchanged for future Soviet Commissar for Foreign Affairs Litvinov, who had been arrested in England.

108. LONSDALE, Gordon [Konon Molody]

SPY: TWENTY YEARS IN SECRET SERVICE: THE MEMOIRS OF GORDON LONSDALE

New York, New York: Hawthorn Books, 1965, pp. 220.

Lonsdale's alleged account of his career in Soviet intelligence, from anti-Nazi underground work to his 1964 exchange for Greville Wynne. A KGB illegal, Lonsdale was convicted and jailed for espionage in the British Portland Naval Secrets Case. The author's views reflect Soviet propaganda and disinformation themes. It has been rumored that this book was edited by Kim Philby.

109. LYSENKO, Vladil Kirillovich

A CRIME AGAINST THE WORLD: MEMOIRS OF A RUSSIAN SEA CAPTAIN

translated from the Russian <u>Mezhdunarodnoye Prestupleniye</u> by Michael Glenny

London, England: Victor Gollancz Ltd., 1983, pp. 254.

Valuable, revealing memoirs of a recent defector from the Soviet Merchant Navy; documents KGB presence in and oversight of the Maritime Fleet for security and for intelligence collection.

110. MANN, Wilfrid Basil

WAS THERE A FIFTH MAN? QUINTESSENTIAL RECOLLECTIONS

Oxford, England: Pergamon Press, 1982, pp. 170.

Chapter X (pp. 113-135) is an effective critique of the Andrew Boyle, Fifth Man story (<u>The Climate of Treason: Five Who Spied for Russia</u>, London, England: Hutchinson, 1979 [q.v.]). Many additional insights into the Philby, MacLean, and Burgess cases.

111. MARCHENKO, Anatoliy

MY TESTIMONY

translated from the Russian <u>Moi Pokazaniia</u> by Michael Scammell

London, England: Pall Mall Press, 1969, pp. 415.

One of the most detailed accounts of the prison and camp system of the post-Stalin era. Provides specifics on the daily camp regimen and the effects of the gradual rehabilitation of both Stalin and the organs of State Security. See pp. 265-266 for a discussion of KGB transfers to other jobs during the Khrushchev period and the later reversal of the process.

112. MARKOV, Georgi

THE TRUTH THAT KILLED

translated by Liliana Brisby

New York, New York: Ticknor and Fields, 1984, pp. 280.

Markov defected from Bulgaria in 1969 and incurred the wrath of Bulgarian Party Chief Zhivkov for broadcasting embarassing information to his homeland. This post-humous autobiography details some of this troublesome information. Markov died in 1978 from an exotic poison now generally attributed to a successful assassination operation by the Bulgarian secret police. As the The New York Times Book Review put it: "The Bulgarian secret service didn't bungle that one, as it would the attempt on the Pope three years later" (8 July 1984).

113. MEDVEDEV, Roy Aleksandrovich

LET HISTORY JUDGE: THE ORIGINS & CONSEQUENCES OF STALINISM

translated by Colleen Taylor and edited by David Joravsky and Georges Haupt

U.S. Edition: New York, New York, Knopf, 1971, pp. 566.

1st Russian Edition: K Sudu Istorii, London, England: Macmillan, 1972, pp. 566.

2nd Russian Edition: K Sudu Istorii: Genezis i Posledstviia Stalinizma, 2nd revised edition, New York: A.A. Knopf, 1974, pp. 1136

Damning account by a prominent Soviet dissident based on unpublished memoirs, interviews and documents of the Stalin period and its aftermath. Useful for its por-trayals of Party and security service personnel, their roles in Stalin's policies, how they were affected by them, and the post-Beria transformation in Party administration and oversight of the KGB.

114. ---------

KHRUSHCHEV

translated by Brian Pearce

U.S. Edition: Garden City, New York: Anchor Press, Doubleday, 1983, pp. 292.

U.K. Edition: Oxford, England: B. Blackwell, 1982, pp. 292.

For the first revelation in print regarding the suicide of the former security service chief, S.N. Kruglov (1956), see p. 114.

115. MEDVEDEV, Zhores Aleksandrovich

ANDROPOV

1st U.S. Edition: New York, New York: W.W. Norton & Co., 1983, pp. 227.

2nd U.S. Edition: Andropov: With A New Afterword, New York, New York: Penguin, 1984, pp. 240.

U.K. Edition: Oxford, England: B. Blackwell, 1983, pp. 227.

Ostensibly critical on Soviet internal developments since Stalin, this presentation is fully supportive of current Soviet views on foreign policy issues.

116. MONAT, Pawel with John DILLIE

SPY IN THE U.S.

New York, New York: Harper and Row, 1962, pp. 208.

A former Polish military attache in Washington reminisces about his intelligence gathering activities in the US and the control of the Polish Service by the Soviets.

117. MUGGERIDGE, Malcolm

LIKE IT WAS: THE DIARIES OF MALCOLM MUGGERIDGE

selected and edited by John Bright-Holmes

U.K. Edition: London, England: Collins, 1981, pp. 560.

U.S. Edition: New York, New York: Wm. Morrow & Co., 1982, pp. 560.

Corrosive insights to many of the notorious figures in British politics since the Thirties. See indexed entries for: Walter Duranty; Guy Burgess; Claude Cockburn; Donald MacLean; Kim Philby; Robert Bruce Lockhart; et. al.

118. MYAGKOV, Aleksei

INSIDE THE KGB

U.S. Edition: New Rochelle, New York: Arlington House, 1976, pp. 131.

U.K. Edition: Richmond, Surrey: Foreign Affairs Publishing Co., 1976, pp. 131.

Reissued by Ballantine Books, New York, New York: 1981, pp. 184.

Captain Myagkov defected to the British in West Berlin in 1974. He is the only living defector from the KGB Counterintelligence element (the Third Chief Director-ate) in the Soviet Armed Forces. This is Myagkov's own account and draws extensively on the unique compilation of KGB notes and directives he brought with him. Some of the latter are reproduced in their entirety; many of the others are worked into the text.

119. NEKIPELOV, Victor

INSTITUTE OF FOOLS: NOTES FROM SERBSKY

edited and translated from the Russian by Marco Carynnyk and Marta Horban

New York, New York: Farrar, Straus, Giroux, 1980, pp. 292.

Discusses the KGB use of psychiatry for political purposes.

120. NYARADI, Nicholas

   MY RINGSIDE SEAT IN MOSCOW

   New York, New York: Crowell, 1953, pp. 307.

Of particular interest is Chapter 9 (pp. 94-106), "A Matter of Intelligence", for insights into the spirit and practice of Soviet security and intelligence, by a former Hungarian representative in Moscow. It is also notable for details on the personality and activity of the former Security chief, V.N. Merkulov.

121. ORLOV, Alexander

   HANDBOOK OF INTELLIGENCE AND GUERILLA WARFARE

   Ann Arbor, Michigan: University of Michigan Press, 1963, pp. 187.

A manual by a former Lieutenant General of the NKVD on the principles and techniques (many still applicable) of clandestine intelligence collection and clandestine warfare as practiced by the Soviets in the 1920s and 1930s. The author defected in 1938 while serving as the NKVD resident in Spain during the Spanish Civil War.

122. ---------

   THE SECRET HISTORY OF STALIN'S CRIMES

   New York, New York: Random House, 1953. pp. 366.

The author was one of the highest-ranking State Security officers to defect to the West. The senior NKVD official resident in Spain during the Civil War, he directed among others the operation removing the Spanish state gold reserves to the USSR. This book was one of the first to direct detailed attention to the nature and extent of the Stalinist purges of the 1930s.

123. OZEROV, Georgiy Aleksandrovich

EN PRISON AVEC TUPOLEV

[In Prison With Tupolev]

French Edition: trad. de N. Krivocheine et M. Gorbov en collaboration avec Nina Nidermiller. Paris, France: A. Michel, 1973, pp. 159.

Yugoslav Edition: A. Sharagin. Tupolevskaya Sharaga (Tupolev's Closed Design Bureau). Belgrade, Yugoslavia: Marin Cudmin Se Slobodon Masic, c. 1971, pp. 125.

Russian Edition: Tupolevskaya Sharaga. Frankfurt am Main, FRG, Posev-Verlag, V Goradich KG, 1973, pp. 125

The published version of what originally had been a samizdat manuscript circulated in the USSR, dealing with one element of the Special Design Bureaus of the State Security's Economic Directorate. Reminiscent of Solzhenitsyn's novel The First Circle--which dealt with the early 1950s--this factual narrative focuses on a "sharaga" set up by Beria in 1938 for the aviation industry.

124. PENKOVSKIY, Oleg

THE PENKOVSKIY PAPERS

translated by Peter Deriabin, introduction and commentary by Frank Gibney, foreword by Edward Crankshaw

U.S. Edition: Garden City, New York: Doubleday & Co., 1965, pp. 411.

French Edition: Carnets d'un Agent Secret, traduit du russe par Peter Deriabin et de l'americain par Paule Ravenel, preface de Constantin Melnik, introduction et commentaires de Frank Gibney, Paris, France: J. Tallandier, 1966, pp. 379.

Reissued by Ballantine Books, New York, New York: 1982, pp. 381.

Includes personal testimony and anecdotal material on Soviet policies and personalities and on Soviet intelligence organization by a GRU colonel recruited by US and British intelligence.

125. PETROV, Vladimir and Evdokia

EMPIRE OF FEAR

U.S. Edition: New York, New York: Frederick Praeger, 1956, pp. 351.

U.K. Edition: London, England: A. Deutsch, 1956, pp. 351.

Both husband and wife were members of Soviet state security when they defected in Australia in 1954. Their book depicts Soviet world-wide espionage activities and the excesses of the purges; the Australian Royal Commission Report was based on the Petrovs' testimony and documentary materials. More recently, the Australian government has released the Petrov papers to the public.

126. PHILBY, Harold A.R. ("Kim")

MY SILENT WAR

1st U.S. Edition: New York, New York: Grove Press, 1968, pp. 262.

2nd U.S. Edition: My Silent War: the Soviet Master Spy's Own Story, New York, New York: Grove Press, 1968, pp. 159.

U.K. Edition: introduction by Graham Greene, London, England: MacGibbon & Kee, 1968, pp. 164.

Reissued by Ballantine Books, New York, New York, 1983, pp. 218.

Philby gives an account of his recruitment at Cambridge and his career as a Soviet agent in the British Intelligence Service. This book was written in Moscow after Philby's defection to the Soviet Union; it has only recently (1980) been made available to readers in the Soviet Union: Moya Tainaya Voyna: Vospominaniya Sovetskogo razvedchika, Moscow, USSR: Voyenizdat, 1980, pp. 191. The same caution as to its disinformational aspects should be used by the reader as was suggested in the comment on the Lonsdale book (q.v.).

127. PODRABINEK, Alexandre

PUNITIVE MEDICINE

translated by Alexandre Lehrman, with a foreword
by Alexander Ginzberg

Ann Arbor, Michigan: Karoma Publishers, 1980, pp.
223.

An indispensable compilation and translation of the
applicable administrative regulations regarding
punitive medicine developed during the 1960s and early
1970s in the USSR.

128. POHL-WANNEMACHER, Helga

**RED SPY AT NIGHT: A TRUE STORY OF ESPIONAGE AND
SEDUCTION BEHIND THE IRON CURTAIN**

translated by Rena Wilson

London, England: New English Library, 1977, pp.
176.

Probably an apocryphal account by a self-declared
Soviet agent who claimed to have defected to the West.

129. PORETSKY, Elizabeth (aka Elsa Bernaut and Elsa
Reiss)

**OUR OWN PEOPLE: A MEMOIR OF IGNACE REISS AND HIS
FRIENDS**

U.S. Edition: Ann Arbor, Michigan: University of
Michigan Press, 1970, pp. 278.

U.K. Edition: London, England: Oxford University
Press, 1969, pp. 278.

French Edition: Les Notres, Paris, France: Denoel
(Les Lettres Nouvelles), 1969, pp. 302.

An authoritative but cautiously worded memoir by the
widow of one of Soviet Military Intelligence's (GRU)
most active and successful illegal agents in the 1920s,
Ignatz Poretsky, better known under his alias, Ignace

Reiss, and his code-name, "Ludwig". Reiss and his boyhood and Service friend Walter Krivitsky (q.v.) were re-activated as illegal operatives in Western Europe in 1933-1934 by the NKVD (the Security Service). The two defected in Paris in 1937 and 1938, respectively, and both were silenced by the NKVD; Reiss by brutal murder in Lausanne, September 5, 1937, and Krivitsky by "suicide"--the author believes, in Washington, D.C., February 10 or 11, 1941. This work is a restrained memorial to her husband and to a small group of his Ukrainian-Polish colleagues who were early victims of the KGB system. In the course of it, she seeks to correct some of the errors which had crept into the Krivitsky story through his ghost writers.

130. RADVANYI, Janos

DELUSION AND REALITY: GAMBITS, HOAXES AND DIPLOMATIC ONE-UPSMANSHIP IN VIETNAM

with a foreword by George W. Ball

South Bend, Indiana: Gateway Editions, Ltd., 1978, pp. 295.

An account by a former senior Hungarian diplomat about Soviet political action, deception and disinformation with particular reference to Vietnam.

131. RASCHHOFER, Hermann

POLITICAL ASSASSINATION: THE LEGAL BACKGROUND OF THE OBERLANDER AND STASHINSKY CASES

translated by Ernst Schlosser

Tubingen, FRG: F. Schlichtenmayer, 1964, pp. 231.

Stashinsky was a KGB professional assassin who defected to West Germany in 1961.

132. ROMANOV, A.I. [pseudonym]

NIGHTS ARE LONGEST THERE: A MEMOIR OF THE SOVIET SECURITY SERVICES

U.S. Edition: Boston, Massachusetts: Little, Brown & Co., 1972, pp. 256.

U.K. Edition: <u>Nights Are Longest There: SMERSH</u>
<u>From The Inside</u>, London, England: Hutchinson,
1972, pp. 256.

A useful account of "SMERSH" training and special
operational groups and missions during World War II and
after in the Ukraine, Poland, Austria, and Hungary. The
author defected in Vienna to the Americans in 1947, and
was re-settled by the British. It offers commentary,
some of it critical of prevailing Western views, about
Soviet Security Service personalities, organization,
and domestic security operations since 1945. The author
was found drowned in London in early 1984.

133. SAKHAROV, Vladimir Nikolvyevich and Umberto TOSI

HIGH TREASON

New York, New York: G.P. Putnam's Sons, 1980, pp.
318.

Reissued by Ballantine Books, New York, New York:
1985, pp. 311.

A thought-provoking autobiography of one of the Soviet
"Golden Youth", a son of the privileged "New Class",
well-connected by multiple family ties with the
Security Service. Sakharov's story, first told by John
Barron in a chapter of his book, <u>KGB</u> (q.v.), emerges
from this more detailed account of his Ministry of
Foreign Affairs career as an Arabic language expert and
KGB co-optee, as a CIA agent in place, and as a new
American troubled by his resettlement handling in the
US.

134. SEJNA, Jan

WE WILL BURY YOU

London, England: Sidgwick and Jackson, 1982, pp.
205.

General Sejna--Assistant Secretary to the Czech Defense
Council, Chief of Staff to the Czech Ministry of
Defense, member of Parliament and member of the Czech
Communist Party Central Committee--is one of the
highest ranking officials to defect from the Soviet
Bloc. This unique access is the basis for his detailed

exposition of the 1960s Soviet Strategic Plan which he maintains set out Moscow's long-term domestic and foreign objectives.

135. SHIFRIN, Avraham

THE FIRST GUIDEBOOK TO PRISONS AND CONCENTRATION CAMPS OF THE SOVIET UNION

U.S. Edition: New York, New York: Bantam Books, 1982, pp. 390.

Russian Edition: Putevoditel'po Lageriam Tiur'mam i Psikhiaricheskm Tiur'mam v SSSR, Uhldingen, Switzerland: Stephanus Edition, 1980, pp. 390.

A more dramatic presentation of Shifrin's information than his testimony before the U.S. Senate Internal Security Sub-committee in the early 1970s. It is also the most encyclopedic compilation of contemporary Gulag data available in print.

136. SIGL, Rupert

IN THE CLAWS OF THE KGB: MEMOIRS OF A DOUBLE AGENT

Philadelphia, Pennsylvania: Dorrance, 1978, pp. 247.

Rich in case details and insights, an important contribution to the literature of Soviet security and intelligence activity. Sigl was recruited by the Soviets in the late 1940s for agent work in his Austrian homeland. Compromised in the early 1950s, he was flown to Moscow, trained, and shifted to agent work in and from East Berlin against American and other targets in West Germany until he defected in 1969.

137. SOLOVYOV, Vladimir and Elena KLEPIKOVA

YURI ANDROPOV: A SECRET PASSAGE INTO THE KREMLIN

translated by Guy Daniels in collaboration with the authors

New York, New York: Macmillan, 1983, pp. 302.

One of a half-dozen biographies to appear within a year of the late General Secretary's accession to power. This account, like Medvedev's and Zemtsov's, offers dramatic though largely unsubstantiated insights (e.g., Andropov as the instigator of the Afghanistan invasion) into the life of the only KGB chief to achieve the pinnacle of Party power.

138. SOLZHENITSYN, Alexandr Isaevich

THE GULAG ARCHIPELAGO, 1918-1956: AN EXPERIMENT IN LITERARY INVESTIGATION

translated from the Russian Arkhipelag Gulag by Thomas P. Whitney (vol. 1 & 2) and Harry Willetts (vol. 3)

New York, New York: Harper & Row, 1974-1976 (three volumes), pp. 660; 712; 558.

"Gulag I" gives the historical background of institutionalized terror established by Lenin and developed by Stalin. "Gulag II" details the primary medium of this terror, the slave labor camps. "Gulag III" is the concluding, and for the non-specialist, the most readable volume of this literary investigation and record of the impact on Russia and the Russians of the Communist Party system. Solzhenitsyn deals here with the Corrective Labor Camps and their State Security (KGB) and Party masters in the period of mature Stalinism (1945-1953) and after. It shows that the breakdown of the Camp regime began before Stalin's death, that the quick structural and other adaptations under Khrushchev were essentially cosmetic and palliative, and that there was a creeping recidivism under Brezhnev and Andropov. The account of the popular rising in the city of Novocherkassk, 2 June 1962, pp. 506-514, has not appeared elsewhere in such detail.

139. SOUVARINE, Boris

STALIN: A CRITICAL SURVEY OF BOLSHEVISM

1st U.S. Edition: New York, New York: Arno Press, 1972, pp. 690.

2nd U.S. Edition: New York, New York: Octagon Books, 1972, pp. 690.

French Edition: <u>Staline: Apercu Historique du Bolschevisme.</u> Paris, France: Editions Champs Libre, 1977, pp. 639.

Updated and enlarged edition of his classic 1935 biography, with a new preface. [See <u>Survey</u> (London), March 1978, pp. 118-131 for translated excerpts from the new preface.]

140. STRAIGHT, Michael

AFTER LONG SILENCE

New York, New York: Norton, 1983, pp. 351.

Apologia by the former editor of <u>The New Republic</u> who was recruited and handled for the Soviets by Anthony Blunt at Cambridge in the mid-1930s. Later, Straight admitted to being handled by a "Michael Green", a Soviet illegal who brought greetings from the "friends" at Cambridge. Straight's connections to Blunt, Guy Burgess, and the Soviets did not surface until the Kennedy years. When offered a job requiring security screening, he volunteered these connections to the FBI which subsequently asked him to talk to the British security service, MI5.

141. SUVOROV, Victor

THE LIBERATORS: MY LIFE IN THE SOVIET ARMY

U.S. Edition: New York, New York: W.W. Norton, 1983, pp. 202.

U.K. Edition: London, England: Hamish Hamilton, 1981, pp. 202.

Anecdotal treatment by a former Soviet military officer on the difficulties of life in the Soviet armed forces. See the last section of the book for a detailed description of the KGB execution of an enlisted deserter in Czechoslovakia in 1968. The techniques described bear close resemblance to the execution style of the 1930s.

142. --------

INSIDE THE SOVIET ARMY

U.S. Edition: Macmillan & Company, 1984, pp. 296.

U.K. Edition: London, England: Hamish Hamilton, 1982, pp. 296.

Suvorov's second work is a handbook on the Soviet Armed Forces. Of particular interest is his description of Military Intelligence (GRU) and its Diversionary or Spetsnaz Troops (Special Purpose Forces).

143. --------

INSIDE SOVIET MILITARY INTELLIGENCE

U.S. Edition: New York, New York: MacMillan Publishing Company, 1984, pp. 193.

U.K. Edition: Soviet Military Intelligence. London, England: Hamish Hamilton, 1984, pp. 193.

While this is one of the rare works ever to appear on Soviet military intelligence (the GRU), its value is somewhat marred by error and uncompelling assertions. For example: People's Control is identified as a secret police organ (p.xi), but it is really a Party body; Kuusinen is rendered as Kusinien (p.12), Vyshinsky as Voyshinski (p.21); the GRU was, in 1935, tasked with purging NKVD overseas organs (p.21); the budget of the GRU is many times greater than that of the KGB because it draws on funds of all Soviet armaments industries and science while the KGB must work from its own budget (p.37). The author appears much more authoritative and balanced in his narrative when he discusses GRU Spetsnaz or special purpose forces (Chapter 7) and Tactical Reconnaissance (Chapter 8). His insider's insights in these chapters make this work a useful addition to the literature.

144. TOLLEY, Kemp

CAVIAR AND COMMISSARS: THE EXPERIENCES OF A U.S. NAVAL OFFICER IN STALIN'S RUSSIA

Annapolis, Maryland: Naval Institute Press, 1983, pp. 320.

Admiral Tolley's long Naval career included service
with the US mission in Moscow during World War II.
This memoir highlights the difficulties created for
US staff personnel by the Security Service.

145. TREPPER, Leopold

**THE GREAT GAME: MEMOIRS OF THE SPY HITLER COULDN'T
SILENCE**

New York, New York: McGraw-Hill, 1977, pp. 442.

The author began his underground work in Palestine and
France in the 20s and the early 30s. In 1938-1939, he
was the founder and leader of the "Red Orchestra", one
of the most-written about and least understood Soviet
networks of the Second World War. Trepper served as an
illegal Resident in Belgium and France for the GRU
(Soviet Military Intelligence). His primary target upon
arrival on post was the United Kingdom. The book is a
monument to the successive errors in Moscow headquarters' operational handling which doomed Trepper and
his colleagues to relatively swift identification and
arrest in 1941-1942. Following the liberation of Paris,
Trepper returned to Moscow (January 1945) where he was
incarcerated for over nine years and finally released.

146. ULANOVSKIY, Nadezhda and Maya

ISTORIA ODNOI SEM'I

[The Story of One Family]

New York, New York: Chalidze Publications, 1982,
pp. 445.

Memoirs by the wife of the GRU illegal, Alexander
Ulanovskiy, who accompanied him to Shanghai in the late
1920s and to the United States in the early 1930s. Now
an emigre, with her daughter in Israel, this story
provides important corroborative detail on the activities of Richard Sorge, Whittaker Chambers and on GRU
illegals in general. See also, Godfrey Blunden, A Room
on the Route (q.v.).

147. VALTIN, Jan (pseudonym of Richard Julius Herman Krebs)

OUT OF THE NIGHT

1st U.S. Edition: New York, New York: Alliance Book Corp., 1941, pp. 841.

2nd U.S. Edition: New York, New York: Alliance Book Corp., 1941, pp. 749.

3rd U.S. Edition: Garden City, New York: Garden City Publishing Co., 1942, pp. 749.

Portuguese Edition: Do Fundo Da Noite; Comintern-Prof-intern-Gestapo-GPU-Scotland Yard... Memorias De Um Famoso Espiao E Agitador Alemao, traducao de R. Mahalhaes Junior e. A.C. Callado, Rio de Janeiro, Brazil: J. Olympio, 1942, pp. 785.

Spanish Edition: La Noche Quedo Atras, Buenos Aires, Argentina: Editorial Claridad, 1942, pp. 695.

The author, a German Spartacist, was an active Communist and Comintern courier, agent, failed assassin, and double-agent abroad in the 1920s and 1930s. This book was a sensation in its day, and was among the very first of its genre. It is important for the light it directs at Ernest Friedrich Wollweber and the operational connections with the Baltic and International Seamen's organizations.

148. VASSALL, William John Christopher

VASSALL: THE AUTOBIOGRAPHY OF A SPY

London, England: Sidgwick and Jackson, 1975, pp. 200.

A frank autobiographic account of a classic KGB homosexual entrapment and recruitment in Moscow during service at the British Embassy.

149. VOSLENSKY, Michael

**NOMENKLATURA: THE SOVIET RULING CLASS—
AN INSIDER'S REPORT**

translated by Eric Mosbacher

Garden City, New York: Doubleday and Company,
Inc., 1984, pp. 455.

Meticulous presentation on how the Soviet dictatorial
elite perpetuates its power and privilege through the
system of Party-directed patronage known as "nomenclatura." Milovan Djilas whose The New Class first
dissected this phenomena, rates this work as among the
best about the Soviet system (from the Preface, p.
xiv). Voslensky sees the KGB and military as the
pillars of the "nomenklatura's" class power.

150. WERNER, Ruth [pseudonym of Ursula Sukcynski]

SONJA'S RAPPORT

German Edition: East Berlin, German Democratic
Republic: Verlag Neues Leben, 1977, pp. 342.

Russian Edition: Moscow, USSR: Progress Publishers, 1980, pp. 264.

The author is Ursula Sukcynski who as "Ursula Ham-
burger" and "Ursula Buerton" worked as a GRU agent and
radio operative in Shanghai (1930-1933, with Richard
Sorge), in North China (1934-1935), in Danzig and
Switzerland (late 1930s). During World War II she
worked in the U.K. where she is said to have handled
contacts with Klaus Fuchs (see Chapman Pincher, Too
Secret Too Long [q.v.]).

151. WYNNE, Greville

CONTACT ON GORKY STREET

New York, New York: Atheneum, 1968, pp. 222.

The British agent's first-hand account, somewhat
colored, of his missions to Moscow to contact Colonel
Oleg Penkovskiy.

152. ‒‒‒‒‒‒‒‒

THE MAN FROM ODESSA

London, England: Hale, 1981, pp. 255.

An autobiographical introduction to Wynne's role in the Penkovskiy case. It also includes new material on a GRU Major, "Sergei Kuznov", who Wynne claims, defected prior to the Penkovskiy affair; details on the last days of the Penkovskiy operation; and new data on the events leading to the crash of the Soviet TU-144 at the Paris Air Show in June 1973. Difficult to cross-check.

153. ZEMSTOV, Ilya

ANDROPOV: POLICY DILEMMAS AND THE STRUGGLE FOR POWER

Jerusalem, Israel: Israel Research Institute of Contemporary Society [IRICS], P.O. Box 687, 91006, Jerusalem), pp. 252.

Provocative analysis in the genre of the Solovyov and Klepikova (q.v.) study mentioned earlier. Zemtsov sees the KGB slowly absorbing the "partocracy", which he feels would be more dangerous, ultimately, to Western interests.

Articles and Chapters

154. ALEXEEV, Kirril Mikhailovich

"WHY I DESERTED THE SOVIET"

Saturday Evening Post 220 (June 26, 1948): pp. 10, 18-9, 24, 99, 101.

"WAS AMBASSADOR OUMANSKY MURDERED?"

Saturday Evening Post 221 (July 3, 1948): pp. 20-1, 94, 96.

"HOW WE DUPED OUR AMERICAN FRIENDS"

Saturday Evening Post 221 (July 10, 1948): pp. 30, 121-2.

Alexeev, the former Soviet Commercial Attache in Mexico, defected to the United States in 1946. His revelations, though sensational, were not given wide attention at the time. They were particularly critical of the Soviet security service Resident in Mexico, Lev Aleksandrovich Tarasov.

155. AMALRIK, Andrei

"WHO ARE THE KGB?"

Far Eastern Economic Review 94 (December 31, 1976), pp. 20-1.

A key question and a response by a political dissident, who was a victim in 1980 of a fatal automobile accident in Western Europe, and who had come to know the system's cutting edge. Amalrik's article is the introduction to the Far Eastern Economic Review's longer treatment of the "KGB in Asia (Part II)", pp. 20-34.

156. ARTEMYEV, Vyacheslav P.

"OKR: STATE SECURITY IN THE SOVIET ARMED FORCES"

In The Soviet Secret Police. Edited by Simon Wolin and Robert M. Slusser

New York, New York: Praeger, 1957, pp. 408.

Artemyev was a graduate of Frunze Military Academy and former officer of Soviet state security. OKR (Otdel Kontrrazvedki-Counterintelligence) is the Third Chief Directorate of the KGB (Counterintelligence in the Armed Forces).

157. AVTORKHANOV, Abdurakhman

"THE SOVIET TRIANGULAR DICTATORSHIP: PARTY, POLICE AND ARMY: FORMATION AND SITUATION"

Ukrainian Quarterly 34 (Summer 1978): pp. 135-53.

An important re-interpretation of a subject taken up in the author's 1966 book (q.v.).

158. BUZEK, Antonin

"DIPLOMACY AND ESPIONAGE"

East Europe 11 (August 1962): pp. 10-11.

The defected ex-chief correspondent in London of the Czech News Agency (CTK) describes agent activity under diplomatic cover during his tenure.

"DIPLOMACY AND ESPIONAGE"

Military Review 43 (January 1963): pp. 85-88.

Describes the Czech service as "in fact, an extension of the Soviet Intelligence Service, used in places where the Soviets cannot penetrate."

159. DEMIDOV, Sasha (pseudonym)

"WIR SCHOSSEN BESSER ALS COWBOYS – DIE AKTIVITAET DES SOWJETISCHEN GEHEIMDIENSTES KGB IN DER TSCHECHOSLOWAKEI"

[We Shot Better Than The Cowboys – The Activities Of The Soviet Secret Service in Czechoslovakia]

Der Spiegel, 20 July 1970, pp. 86-87, 90-91, 93.

The author is a former Czech military intelligence officer who defected to the West in October 1969. These are detailed revelations, based on personal participation, about the KGB security forces and Demidov's active role in the preparation and execution of specific operational measures, with the cooperation of selected Czech cadres, during the occupation of Czechoslovakia by Warsaw Pact troops in 1968.

160. DERIABIN, Peter and Frank GIBNEY

"RED AGENT'S VIVID TALES OF TERROR"

Life, 23 March 1959, pp. 110-12, 114, 116, 119, 120.

"KREMLIN INTRIGUE AND DEBAUCHERY"

Life, 30 March 1959, pp. 80-85, 87-88, 90.

A two part expose of the KGB Residentura chiefs and some of their agents in Vienna, and in the Moscow headquarters.

161. DZIRKVELOV, Ilya

"HOW THE KGB OPERATES: ANSWERS FROM A KGB DEFECTOR"

Interview by Leonid Finkelstein

Intelligence Report. (Standing Committee on Law and National Security, American Bar Association) 3 (July 1981): pp. 3-6.

Dzirkvelov defected to the British in Geneva in May 1980. He joined the KGB early in World War II and says he left it in 1956 for media work until he defected.

162. GLAZOV, Yuri

"THE PASSING OF A YEAR...: THE RUSSIAN WORLD VIEW FROM AMERICA"

Studies in Soviet Thought 15 (December 1975): pp. 273-290.

163. KRASIN, Victor

"HOW I WAS BROKEN BY THE KGB"

translated by Antonina W. Bovis

The New York Times Magazine, 18 March 1984, pp. 54-57.

Adapted from Krasin's The Trial published in Russian (Chalidze Publications, New York, 1983). Account of contemporary KGB tactics for extracting confessions and compromising the subject.

164. KRIVITSKY, Walter G. [Samuel Ginzburg]

"STALIN'S HAND IN SPAIN"

Saturday Evening Post 211 (April 15, 1939): pp. 5-7, 115-22.

"WHY STALIN SHOT HIS GENERALS"

Saturday Evening Post 211 (April 22, 1939): pp. 16-17, 71-74, 76-77.

"STALIN APPEASES HITLER"

Saturday Evening Post 211 (April 29, 1939): pp. 12-13, 84-89.

"WHY DID THEY CONFESS?"

Saturday Evening Post 212 (June 17, 1939): pp. 5-6, 96-8, 100-1.

"MY FLIGHT FROM STALIN"

Saturday Evening Post 212 (August 5, 1939): pp. 7, 73-74, 76-80.

"WHEN STALIN COUNTERFEITED DOLLARS"

Saturday Evening Post 212 (September 30, 1939): pp. 8-9, 80-4.

"THE GREAT RED FATHER"

Saturday Evening Post 212 (November 4, 1939): pp. 12-3, 66-8, 72-5.

"THE RED ARMY: AUXILIARY OF GERMANY'S MILITARY MIGHT"

Saturday Evening Post 212 (June 1, 1940): pp. 9-10, 91-4, 96.

165. KUZNETSOV, Anatoliy

"RUSSIAN WRITERS AND THE SECRET POLICE"

In Man, State, and Society in the Soviet Union. Edited by Joseph L. Nogee

New York, New York: Praeger, 1972, pp. 599.

Details the writer's own experiences with the KGB,
beginning with the attempt to co-opt his services for a
trip abroad.

166. MYAGKOV, Aleksei

   "CONFESSIONS OF A KGB OFFICER"

   Soviet Analyst 6 (January 13, 1977): pp. 5-7.

   "THE ROLE OF THE KGB IN WORLD AFFAIRS"

   Foreign Affairs Research Institute, April 1977,
   pp. 6.

167. ORIONOVA, Galina

   "ESCAPE FROM BOREDOM: A DEFECTOR'S STORY"

   Interview by Nora Beloff

   Atlantic, November 1980, pp. 42-50.

On the propaganda and foreign influence role of
Arbatov's Institute for the Study of the United States
and Canada by a former staffer. Discusses the KGB
connection.

   **"INTERVIEW GIVEN BY FIRST DEFECTOR FROM ARBATOV'S
   AMERICAN INSTITUTE'"**

   Interview by Leonid Finkelstein

   Intelligence Report. (Standing Committee on Law
   and National Security, American Bar Association) 3
   (September 1981): pp. 6-8.

168. ORLOV, Alexander

   "GHASTLY SECRETS OF STALIN'S POWERS"

   Life, (6 April 1953), pp. 10-12, 115-23; (13 April
   1953), pp. 160-62, 164, 166, 168, 170; (20 April
   1953), pp. 142-44, 146, 148, 150, 153, 154, 156,
   159; (20 April 1953), pp. 145-46, 148-52, 157-58,
   respectively.

See The Secret History of Stalin's Crimes (q.v.).

"THE BERIA I KNEW"

Life, 20 July 1953, pp. 33, 35-36.

In 1925 the author was commander of OGPU frontier troops in Transcaucasia. There he first met Lavrenti Beria, a young officer in the Tblisi OGPU. From his vantage point Orlov was in a position to observe the beginning of Beria's rise.

169. RASTVOROV, Lt. Col. Yuri Aleksandrovich

"HOW RED TITANS FOUGHT FOR SUPREME POWER"

Life, 29 November 1954, pp. 18-21, 146-56.

"RED FRAUD AND INTRIGUE IN THE FAR EAST"

Life, 6 December 1954, pp. 174-92.

"GOODBYE TO RED TERROR"

Life, 13 December 1954, pp. 49-58.

The author defected to US authorities in Japan in January 1954 after eleven years in the Security Service, four and a half years of it in the Tokyo Residency. These articles provide insights into political developments in Moscow, to the policy background of initiation of the Korean War, and the maturing of his plans for defection.

170. SCHUMAN, Tomas [pseudonym]

"NO 'NOVOSTY' IS GOOD NOVOSTY. NOVOSTY PRESS AGENCY: AN EXTENSION OF THE SOVIET PROPAGANDA AND SUBVERSION SYSTEM."

World Peace & Freedom Monthly 1 (June 1978), re-named Our Canada [Toronto, Canada] 1 (July 1978): pp. 13.

The author is a former Novosty Press Agency (APN) employee who worked for the Information Department of the Soviet Embassy in India before his defection there in 1970. This is a booklet published in tabloid format in a Toronto, Canada publication, known initially as World Peace & Freedom Monthly which re-titled with its seventh issue, Our Canada.

171. SHOSTAKOVICH, Maxim

    "CONVERSATIONS WITH THE KGB"

    Washington Post, 29 November 1981, pp. C1, 5.

Translated text of a taped conversation between Shostakovich and an apparent KGB officer who was accompanying his orchestra. This took place at a West German police station following Shostakovich's defection in April 1980. A classic confrontation.

172. SIMIS, Konstantin

    "RUSSIA'S UNDERGROUND MILLIONAIRES...HOW TO SUCCEED IN BUSINESS WHERE BUSINESS IS A CRIME"

    Fortune, 29 June 1981, pp. 36-42, 47, 50.

173. THAYER, Charles W.

    "MVD MAN'S DECLARATION OF INDEPENDENCE"

    Life, 5 July 1954, pp. 69-72, 75-6, 78-80.

The biography of Lt. Col. Grigori Stepanovich Burlutski, who defected in June 1953 from the 2nd Battalion of the 68th Border Guard Division, MVD, Soviet Turkestan.

174. VOINOVICH, Vladimir

    "PROISSHESTVIE V 'METROPOLE'"

    [Incident At The Metropol]

    Kontinent, No. 5, 1975, pp. 51-97.

Voinovich charges that the KGB attempted to poison him at the Metropol Hotel in Moscow.

175. VOLKMAN, Ernest and Vladimir SAKHAROV

"YURI ANDROPOV.   THE SPY WHO CAME IN FROM THE COLD"

<u>Penthouse</u>, March 1983, pp. 56, 58, 146, 149ff.

Section Four

Secondary Accounts

Books

176. ADELMAN, Jonathan, ed.

TERROR AND COMMUNIST POLITICS: THE ROLE OF THE
SECRET POLICE IN COMMUNIST STATES

Boulder, Colorado: Westview Press, 1984, pp. 292.

This collection of case studies builds on Dallin's and
Breslauer's 1971 Political Terror in Communist Systems
(q.v.) and follows the latter's efforts to develop a
"theoretical literature on political terror" (See
Robert Slusser's critique "Aspects of Political
Terror", Studies in Comparative Communism 5 (Winter
1972): pp. 428-433). Contributions to the present
volume range from Dallin's "Terror in Communist
Regimes" ("...the whole phenomenon of 'routinized
terror' needs rethinking") to a piece on the politics
of education in the PRC, to sections on the Polish,
Soviet, Romanian, Czechoslovak, Hungarian and Cambodian
secret police. The secret police of East Germany,
Albania, Yugoslavia, Mongolia, the PRC, Vietnam, North
Korea and Cuba are omitted; no reasons are offered. The
fixation of analyzing the secret police in the light of
extant Western political-science theories results in
over-conceptualization and misses the central operative
reality of communist systems: the police are action
arms of the Party, the two fused in a fashion making
independent survival impossible.

177. ARMSTRONG, John A., ed.

SOVIET PARTISANS IN WORLD WAR II

foreword by Philip E. Mosely

71

Madison, Wisconsin: University of Wisconsin Press, 1964, pp. 792.

Chapter V, "The Partisan in Soviet Intelligence", which describes Soviet intelligence and security as an instrument of control, as well as a participant in partisan operations, is of particular interest. The entire volume is valuable for students of guerilla warfare.

178. BACKER, George

THE DEADLY PARALLEL: STALIN AND IVAN THE TERRIBLE

New York, New York: Random House, 1950, pp. 240.

Develops parallels between the Security Service under Stalin and the Oprichnina of Ivan IV.

179. BAILEY, Geoffrey [pseudonym]

THE CONSPIRATORS

New York, New York: Harper, 1960, pp. 306.

See pages 3-132 for details on Soviet State Security's "Trust" operation (1921-1927) and its aftermath. The book also includes coverage of the kidnapping of Generals Kutyepov and Miller in the 1930s, and of the Tukhachevskiy Affair of 1937. One of the better and reliable works on the "Trust" and other Soviet operations against the emigration.

180. BARKER, Wayne G. and Rodney E. KAUFMAN

THE ANATOMY OF TWO TRAITORS: THE DEFECTIONS OF BERNON F. MITCHELL AND WILLIAM H. MARTIN

Laguna Hills, California: Aegean Press, 1981.

Mitchell and Martin were NSA employees who defected to the USSR via Mexico and Cuba in June 1960. Both men apparently had contacted the Soviets earlier during an unauthorized trip to Cuba in December 1959. In

September 1960, they surfaced at a ninety minute press conference in Moscow's House of Journalists where they charged the US with carrying out provocative intelligence collection activities against the USSR as well as US allies.

181. BARRON, John

   KGB: THE SECRET WORK OF SOVIET SECRET AGENTS

   New York, New York: Reader's Digest Press, 1974, pp. 462.

A cogent and persuasive account of major cases with valuable details on KGB organization, it combines a popular writing style with significant biographic data and KGB training material on the recruitment of Americans. Almost exclusive coverage of KGB organization and foreign operations comes at the expense of the KGB domestic mission. Unfortunately, the brief appendix on the GRU relegates that service to the position of "subsidiary of the KGB". While the GRU, like the rest of the Soviet military, is penetrated and watched by the KGB's 3rd Chief Directorate, the GRU nonetheless remains the intelligence service of the General Staff and Ministry of Defense.

Together with its sequel, KGB Today, they remain the best works available in their field.

182. --------

   KGB TODAY: THE HIDDEN HAND

   New York, New York: Reader's Digest Press, 1983, pp. 489.

A solid continuation of the factual tradition established by the author with KGB in 1974. Benefits from the recent insights of a former KGB illegal, a Soviet U.N. official and a KGB staffer from the Tokyo residency expert in "active measures." Two appendices include: (1) a continuation of his earlier list of Soviet officials expelled or withdrawn from foreign parts because of espionage or subversive activities; and (2) a discussion of the updated organizational breakdown of the central KGB structure.

183. ---------

MiG PILOT: LT. VICTOR BELENKO'S FINAL ESCAPE

New York, New York: Reader's Digest Press, 1980, pp. 224.

Barron presents an empathetic account of the events leading to Lt. Belenko's defection in a MiG-25 Foxbat in 1976 and the subsequent traumas of his resettlement in the US. Though he was not an intelligence officer, Belenko's experiences provide useful insights into Soviet internal security measures vis-a-vis the military. The difficulties of his adjustment to an open society are not unlike those of previous generations of defectors from the Soviet system.

184. BARRY, Donald D.; William E. BUTLER; and George GINSBURGS, eds.

CONTEMPORARY SOVIET LAW: ESSAYS IN HONOR OF JOHN N. HAZARD

The Hague, Netherlands: Martinus Nijhoff, 1974, pp. 242.

See especially: Juviler, "Criminal Law and Social Control"; Feldbrugge, "Law and Political Dissent in the Soviet Union"; and Loeber, "Samizdat under Soviet Law", for useful surveys of topics close to security service interests and operations.

185. BAUER, Raymond A.

NINE SOVIET PORTRAITS

with the assistance of Edward Wasiolek

Cambridge, Massachusetts: Technology Press of Massachusetts Institute of Technology jointly with Wiley, New York, New York, 1955, pp. 190.

The "Case Study" chapter on the Secret Police operative is a lucid account of the psychology of recruitment, compromise and capture during the Stalin epoch.

186. BEICHMAN, Arnold and Mikhail S. BERNSTAM

ANDROPOV, NEW CHALLENGE TO THE WEST: A POLITICAL BIOGRAPHY

with an introduction by Robert Conquest

New York, New York: Stein & Day, 1983, pp. 255.

Of the half-dozen works to appear during the short tenure of Andropov as Party Chief, this study seems to hold up the best. It lacks most of the idiosyncrasies of several of the others and, as The Christian Science Monitor reviewer put it, "...the authors have also done a better job than their competition in reconstructing Andropov's climb to the top, particularly his brief slippage in the wake of Stalin's passing".

187. BELOFF, Nora

INSIDE THE SOVIET EMPIRE: THE MYTH AND THE REALITY

New York, New York: Times Books, 1980, pp. 188.

The former Observer, Reuters, and Economist correspondent reports on a 5000 km auto trip from Hungary to Tblisi and return. For a trenchant description of encounters with the KGB, see pp. 168-180, Chapter 16.

188. BERNIKOW, Louise

ABEL

New York, New York: Trident Press, 1970, pp. 347.

Reissued by Ballantine Books with a new perspective by the author, New York, New York: 1982, pp. 306.

In this story of the career of Colonel Rudolf Abel, the author conveys a neighbor's insight into Abel's enigmatic personality and Soviet clandestine modus operandi.

189. BINYON, Michael

LIFE IN RUSSIA

New York, New York: Pantheon, 1983, pp. 247.

Recollections and anecdotes by the The Times (London) correspondent in Moscow from 1972 to 1982. Includes some two dozen references regarding the KGB that are both relevant and insightful.

190. BIRMAN, Igor

SECRET INCOMES OF THE SOVIET STATE BUDGET

The Hague, Netherlands: Martinus Nijhoff, 1981, pp. 315; distributed by Kluwer of Boston, Massachusetts.

Birman attempts to calculate the state expenditures on the KGB and the MVD. See Appendix E, pp. 268-271.

191. BLACKSTOCK, Paul W.

THE SECRET ROAD TO WORLD WAR II: SOVIET VERSUS WESTERN INTELLIGENCE, 1921-1939

Chicago, Illinois: Quadrangle Books, Inc., 1969, pp. 384.

Covers much of the operational ground of the 1920s and 1930s described in Geoffrey Bailey's work, The Conspirators (q.v.). It does not, however, significantly expand the documentary or other data about the Soviet security services' unremitting contest with the Russian emigres and various European secret services. Significantly different interpretations exist between the two treatments, which are unresolvable on the basis of existing evidence.

192. BLOBAUM, Robert

FELIX DZIERZYNSKI AND THE SDKPIL: A STUDY OF THE ORIGINS OF POLISH COMMUNISM

Boulder, Colorado: East European Monographs, No. 154, 1984.

Concentrates on Dzerzhinskiy's involvement in the early years of the Social Democratic Party of the Kingdom of Poland and Lithuania.

193. BLOCH, Sidney and Peter REDDAWAY

PSYCHIATRIC TERROR: HOW SOVIET PSYCHIATRY IS USED TO SUPPRESS DISSENT

New York, New York: Basic Books, 1977, pp. 510.

A source-book description of the Soviet use of psychiatry to control dissent. It demonstrates how dissidents were placed in mental hospitals in an effort to intimidate them and keep them quiet.

194. BLOCH-MORHANGE, Jacques

OPERATION FECHTELER

preface par L'Admiral Castex

Paris, France: Editions Jean-Claude, 1953, pp. 115.

This was an attempt to justify a celebrated anti-US Navy forgery which owed its placement and thrust in French media to Bloch-Morhange. The author's informational tip-sheet, Information et Conjectures, was the first to mention the alleged Fechteler report in its issue of February 16, 1952. It argued that the US denial of the authenticity of the Fechteler report was proof that the report was authentic.

195. BLUNDEN, Godfrey

A ROOM ON THE ROUTE

Philadelphia, Pennsylvania: Lippincott Company, 1947, pp. 327.

A fictionalized account of the Ulanovskiys, and Blunden's relationship to Mrs. Ulanovskiy, when she worked with American journalists in Moscow in the mid 1940s.

196. BOCCA, Geoffrey

THE MOSCOW SCENE

New York, New York: Stein & Day, 1976, pp. 192.

See Chapter 7, "Moscow's Swinging Spies" (on Novosti News Agency, for which the author was a short-term consultant), and Chapter 8, "Whatever Happened to Philby & Co" (pp. 95-122). The KGB, according to Bocca, "in many ways...is one of the most cultured and tolerant organizations in the Soviet Union" (p. 97).

197. BOCHENSKI, Joseph and Gerhart NIEMEYER, eds.

HANDBOOK ON COMMUNISM

translation of <u>Handbuch des Weltkommunismus.</u>

New York, New York: Praeger, 1962, pp. 686.

See especially Chapter IX, "Crime and Punishment Under the Soviet Regime", by David J. Dallin, for coverage on the police and punitive measures.

198. BORCKE, Astrid von

DIE URSPRUNGE DES BOLSCHEVISMUS: DIE JAKOBINISCH TRADITION IM RUSSLAND UND DIE THEORIE DER REVO-LUTIONAREN DIKTATUR

[The Sources of Bolshevism: The Jacobin Tradition in Russia and the Theory of Revolutionary Dictatorship]

Munich, FRG: Berchmans, 1977, pp. 646.

199. BOOKER, Christopher

THE GAMES WAR: A MOSCOW JOURNAL

U.S. Edition: Boston, Massachusetts: Faber & Faber, 1981, pp. 236.

U.K. Edition: London, England: Faber & Faber, 1981, pp. 236.

A journalistic account by the Daily Mail (London) special correspondent of the highlights of the Soviet handling of the Olympic games, 1980. Identifies Aleksandre Gres'ko, [Deputy Chief of the Foreign Administration of the USSR Committee for Physical Culture and Sports], as the senior KGB officer on the Soviet Olympic Committee (p. 34).

200. BORNSTEIN, Joseph

THE POLITICS OF MURDER

New York, New York: Sloane, 1951, pp. 295.

An early but still useful background treatment of four Soviet Security "executive action" episodes in the 20s, 30s, and 40s: the Paris kidnappings of emigre Generals Alexander Kutyepov and Eugene Miller (pp. 74-94) in 1930 and 1937, respectively; the liquidation of the defecting NKVD illegal resident, Ignace Reiss (pp. 186-203), also in 1937; and the assassination of Trotsky, in Mexico City in 1941 (pp. 204-237). Marred by the absence of documentation.

201. BOYLE, Andrew

THE FOURTH MAN: THE DEFINITIVE ACCOUNT OF KIM PHILBY, GUY BURGESS AND DONALD MACLEAN AND WHO RECRUITED THEM TO SPY FOR RUSSIA

U.S. Edition: New York, New York: Dial Press, 1979, pp. 504.

U.K. Edition: The Climate of Treason: Five Who Spied for Russia, London, England: Hutchinson, 1979, pp. 504.

The author deals with the cases of the British Foreign Office and intelligence officers Philby, Maclean, and Burgess as Soviet spies, while indicating that there were "fourth" and "fifth" men, and perhaps more in their net. The book led to the public exposure of Anthony Blunt, formerly a war-time member of the British Security Service, a distinguished art historian and Surveyor of the Queen's Pictures.

202. BROOK-SHEPHERD, Gordon

THE STORM PETRELS: THE FLIGHT OF THE FIRST SOVIET DEFECTORS

U.S. Edition: New York, New York: Harcourt, Brace, Jovanovich, 1978, pp. 241.

Reissued by Ballantine Books, New York, New York: 1982, pp. 243.

U.K. Edition: The Storm Petrels: The First Soviet Defectors, 1928-1938, London, England: Collins, 1977, pp. 257.

An account of early Soviet defectors from 1928 until the beginning of World War II. The book commences with the defection of Boris Bajanov, personal assistant to Stalin and Secretary to the Politburo. Bajanov, still living in France at the time of publication, defected in 1928 and was interviewed extensively by Brook-Shepherd. The four other major defectors described are Grigory Bessedovsky, Georges Agabekov, Walter Krivitsky, and Alexander Orlov. Their story, and the stories of other defectors, are intertwined throughout the book.

203. CARRERE D'ENCAUSSE, Helene

CONFISCATED POWER: HOW SOVIET RUSSIA REALLY WORKS

translated from the French Le Pouvoir Confisque by George Holoch

New York, New York: Harper & Row, 1982, pp. 401.

A generally promising analysis on Party, State and Society in the Soviet Union is seriously weakened in its impact by a poor and factually flawed section on the KGB: "...political reality does not at all confirm...that the ...KGB is a central element of the system" (p. 190); "...they [the KGB] are without resources in the face of the central authorities. They are a tool for maintaining order but certainly not active participants in the political system" (p. 193); KGB First Deputy Chairman Tsinev spelled as Tsvinen; General Matrosov spelled as Morozov; some KGB duties blithely ascribed to the MVD.

204. CAVE BROWN, Anthony and Charles B. MACDONALD

ON A FIELD OF RED: THE COMMUNIST INTERNATIONAL AND
THE COMMING OF WORLD WAR II

New York, New York: G.P. Putnam's Sons, 1981, pp.
718.

A grand tour of political action and espionage operations of the Comintern and Soviet intelligence
services, and their roles in the events leading to
World War II. Despite dust jacket claims to new
sources of information, no significant reinterpre-
tations emerge.

205. CHECINSKI, Michael

THE ARMAMENT ADMINISTRATION OF SOVIET BLOCK
STATES: ORGANIZATION AND FUNCTION

Koln, FRG: Bundesinstituts fur Ostwissenschaft-
liche und Internationale Studien, 1979, pp. 32.

(Special Publication of the Federal Institute for
Eastern Economics and International Studies).

See Section 7: "The KGB in the Military-Industrial
Complex" (pp. 26-28). Seldom discussed, this is a
useful, if brief, treatment by a knowledgeable Polish
emigre who served in Polish Military Counterintelligence.

206. CONQUEST, Robert

THE GREAT TERROR: STALIN'S PURGE OF THE THIRTIES

1st U.S. Edition: New York, New York: MacMillan,
1968, pp. 633.

2nd U.S. Edition: New York, New York: MacMillan,
1973, pp. 844.

U.K. Edition: London, England: MacMillan, 1968,
pp. 633.

A study of the Soviet purges of the 1930s by one of the
most respected scholars of the Soviet system. Of

interest is the well-documented coverage of the role played by Soviet state security in Stalin's attack on his own system.

207. --------, ed.

THE SOVIET POLICE SYSTEM

U.S. Edition: New York, New York: Praeger, 1968, pp. 103.

U.K. Edition: London, England: Bodley Head, 1968, pp. 103.

A basic and indespensible survey of the development of the KGB, largely in its domestic aspects, up to 1960.

208. DALLIN, Alexander and George W. BRESLAUER

POLITICAL TERROR IN COMMUNIST SYSTEMS

Stanford, California: Stanford University Press, 1970, pp. 172.

Without having made even a preliminary examination of the organization, development and methodology of the security services, this study makes inferences regarding their diminished contemporary and future status.

209. DALLIN, David J.

SOVIET ESPIONAGE

New Haven, Connecticut: Yale University Press, 1955, pp. 558.

An authoritative source on Soviet espionage operations and systems, the book provides comprehensive treatment of the subject for the period prior to the mid-fifties. It is organized chronologically, with the main pre-World War II and wartime targets of Soviet espionage discussed with material on: France, Germany, Switzerland, Belgium and Holland. Next comes the postwar era and the emergence of the United States as the "main enemy" and target, the role of Soviet satellite services, and discussion of espionage activities in Central Europe. Least effective is the coverage of Soviet espionage and penetration in the United Kingdom.

210. DALLIN, David J. and Boris I. NICOLAEVSKY

FORCED LABOR IN SOVIET RUSSIA

1st U.S. Edition: New Haven, Connecticut: Yale University Press, 1947, pp. 331.

2nd U.S. Edition: New York, New York: Octagon Books, 1974, pp. 331.

1st German Edition: Zwangsarbeit in Sowjetrussland, Deutsche ubertragung von Victor Brougmann, Wien, FRG: Verlag Neue Welt, 1947, pp. 293.

2nd German Edition: Arbeiter Oder Ausgebautete; Das System Der Arbeitslager in Sowjetrussland, Munich, FRG: Neue Zeitung, 1948, pp. 153, "excerpts."

Norwegian Edition: Slavearbeid i Sovjet-Russland, med forlagets etterord og opplysninger og med bilag av Andrei Vysjinski, til Norsk ved Louise Bohr Nilsen, Oslo, Norway: 1948, pp. 294.

Among the first formal authoritative studies of the GULAG system widely published abroad. A necessary source book and point-of-departure for any inquiry into the prison and camp structure of the USSR.

211. DEACON, Richard [pseudonym of Donald McCormick]

A HISTORY OF THE RUSSIAN SECRET SERVICE

U.S. Edition: New York, New York: Taplinger Publishing Co., 1972, pp. 568.

U.K. Edition: London, England: Muller, 1972, pp. 568.

A highly selective, anecdotal survey of the Russian and Soviet security services from the Oprichnina, through the Third Section, the Okhrana, and the Cheka, to the

KGB. Actually not a "history", this is a book by a London journalist who relies largely on secondary materials, on unaccredited "insider" information, and on the Soviet and Western press. "Few sources are given, and distinction is not made between the 'five star' (certain) and the 'one star' (highly dubious) stories" (The Economist, 3 June 1972, p. 59). A basic flaw is the dismissal of Soviet military intelligence, the GRU, from any organizational or operational attention.

212. DEAKIN, Frederick William Dampier and Richard G. STORRY

THE CASE OF RICHARD SORGE

U.S. Edition: New York, New York: Harper and Row, 1966, pp. 373.

U.K. Edition: London, England: Chatto & Windus, 1966, pp. 373.

German Edition: Richard Sorge. Die Geschichte Eines Grossen Doppelspiels, aus dem Englischen von Ulrike von Puttkamer, mit 15 abbildungen auf tafeln, karte von Jutta Winter, Munich, FRG: Piper, 1965, pp. 430.

The story of the leading GRU operative in China and Japan prior to and during early World War II by two distinguished Oxford scholars. Allen Dulles called it "the most authoritative book on one of the greatest spy rings in modern history." It is very well documented.

213. DEDIJER, Vladimir

TITO

1st U.S. Edition: New York, New York: Simon & Schuster, 1953, pp. 443.

2nd U.S. Edition: New York, New York: Arno Press, 1972, pp. 443; reprint.

This was Tito's authorized biography. See p. 255 for one of the most quotable quotes on the security service in the USSR:

"During the past fifteen years [i.e., since 1938] an important role has been acquired by the intelligence service, the NKVD. Instead of a weapon to fight counterrevolution, it has grown into a force in itself; instead of being an instrument of the revolution, it has become a power above Soviet society. The entire activity of the country, the Party, the whole foreign policy--all rests upon the intelligence service; its reports are given priority, it really rules the country."

214. DINERSTEIN, Herbert Samuel

WAR AND THE SOVIET UNION: NUCLEAR WEAPONS AND THE REVOLUTION IN SOVIET MILITARY AND POLITICAL THINKING

1st U.S. Edition: New York, New York: Praeger, 1959, pp. 268.

2nd U.S. Edition: New York, New York: Praeger, 1962, pp. 268 (revised).

Of special interest are pp. 9, 36-47, 49-51, 180-212, which deal with Soviet doctrine on surprise.

215. DONOVAN, James Britt

STRANGERS ON A BRIDGE: THE CASE OF COLONEL ABEL

with a foreword by Charles S. Osmond

New York, New York: Atheneum, 1964, pp. 432.

The lawyer who defended Rudolph Abel and then nego- tiated the exchange of Abel for Francis Gary Powers narrates his experiences with the famous Soviet illegal.

216. DOUGLASS, Joseph D. and Amoretta M. HOEBER

SOVIET STRATEGY FOR NUCLEAR WAR

with a foreword by Eugene V. Rostow

Stanford, California: Hoover Institution Press, 1979, pp. 138.

Based in large measure on a close reading of the Soviet publication, now declassified, Voyennaya Mysl',- (Military Thought). See also the index entries under "Surprise", "Deception", "Disinformation", "KGB", and "Andropov."

217. DUHAMEL, Morvan

DUEL D'ESPIONS POUR UN MIRAGE

[Spies Duel for a Mirage]

Paris, France: Editions France-Empire, 1971, pp. 220.

A most informative case study of an ill-starred GRU attempt to secure a Mirage airplane through a suborned (but doubled) Lebanese pilot-agent.

218. DULLES, Allen Welsh

THE CRAFT OF INTELLIGENCE

New York, New York: Harper & Row, 1963, pp. 277.

A basic work on the subject. The author's background and extensive experience in intelligence gave him unique insight and make for a very readable book. His discussion of counterintelligence and defectors is especially useful.

219. DVORNIK, Francis

ORIGINS OF INTELLIGENCE SERVICES: THE ANCIENT NEAR EAST, PERSIA, GREECE, ROME, BYZANTIUM, THE ARAB MUSLIM EMPIRES, THE MONGOL EMPIRE, CHINA, MUSCOVY

New Brunswick, New Jersey: Rutgers University Press, 1974, pp. 334.

A scholarly work, begun in part for a postwar project
initiated by General William J. Donovan as a private
citizen. Its treatment of the historical antecedents of
the Soviet services is particularly well done.

220. EBON, Martin

THE ANDROPOV FILE: THE LIFE AND IDEAS OF YURI V.
ANDROPOV, GENERAL SECRETARY OF THE CPSU

New York, New York: McGraw Hill, 1983, pp. 284.

An assembly from the public literature, with some
incisive commentary. Nearly half (132 pages) of the
content consists of texts from speeches and articles.

221. EDWARDS, Robert and Kenneth DUNNE

A STUDY OF A MASTER SPY, ALLEN DULLES

London, England: Housemans, 1961, pp. 79.

This attack on Allen Dulles may be an example of
KGB-directed disinformation.

222. EPSTEIN, Edward Jay

LEGEND: THE SECRET WORLD OF LEE HARVEY OSWALD

New York, New York: Reader's Digest Press, 1978,
pp. 382.

This controversial book presents the author's view of
Oswald as a possible KGB agent in the assassination of
President Kennedy. It includes lengthy consideration of
the possibility that the Soviet defector, Yuri Nosenko,
and "Fedora" (the FBI's Soviet agent in the U.N. in New
York) were actually disinformants dispatched to clear
Oswald of KGB connections. The bona fides of Nosenko
are still the subject of debate among students of
Soviet deception operations.

223. FAINSOD, Merle

HOW RUSSIA IS RULED

2nd Edition: Cambridge, Massachusetts: Harvard University Press, 1963, pp. 684.

A classic text. Of special note is Chapter XIII, "Terror as a System of Power", and the footnotes on pages 649-652.

224. FINDER, Joseph

RED CARPET: THE CONNECTION BETWEEN THE KREMLIN AND AMERICA'S MOST POWERFUL BUSINESSMEN - ARMAND HAMMER, AVERELL HARRIMAN, CYRUS EATON, DAVID ROCKEFELLER, DONALD KENDALL

New York, New York: Holt. Rinehart and Winston, 1983, pp. 372.

An incisive and disturbing analysis of the interaction between the Soviet regime and a favored and select group of prominent U.S. businessmen cum public figures. It spans virtually the full tenure of the Soviet system and explores the influence and role of these men in international politics.

225. "FRANCOIS" [pseudonym]

LA 6 COLONNE: ROMAN SANS FICTION

[The Sixth Column: A Non-Fictional Novel]

Paris, France: Stock, 1979, pp. 379.

This is a fictionalised portrayal of Soviet utilization of special purpose and underground shock forces in a future conflict in Europe.

226. FREEMANTLE, Brian

KGB

New York, New York: Holt, Rinehart and Winston, 1982, pp. 192.

A popularly written survey, with excellent photo accompaniment by a British journalist. Marred by serious factual errors; among others: the identification of the FBI source in New York, "Fedora", as the former Soviet diplomat at the United Nations, Lessiovsky (p. 124), and the description of the International Information Department of the Central Committee, CPSU as "an entirely new KGB division" (p.131).

227. FRIEDRICH, Carl Joachim and Zbigniew K. BRZEZINSKI

TOTALITARIAN DICTATORSHIP AND AUTOCRACY

2nd Edition, revised by Carl J. Friedrich: Cambridge, Massachusetts: Harvard University Press, 1965, pp. 439.

See Chapter 14: "The Secret Police and the People's Enemies" (pp. 172-182) and Chapter 15: "Purges, Confessions, and Camps" (pp. 183-202).

228. FULLER, William C., Jr.

"THE INTERNAL TROOPS OF THE MVD SSSR", THE COLLEGE STATION PAPERS: NO. 6

College Station, Texas: 1983, pp. 49.

A joint publication of Defense Studies, University of Edinburgh, Scotland and the Center for Strategic Technology, The Texas Engineering Experiment Station of the Texas A & M University System.

A useful, critical study of the origins, history, present status and missions of a most important element of security service armed forces; solidly based on the major Russian-language materials.

229. GARDER, Michel

L'AGONIE DU REGIME EN RUSSIE SOVIETIQUE

[The Agony of the Regime in Soviet Russia]

French Edition: Paris, France: La Table Ronde, 1965, pp. 206.

German Edition: <u>Die Agonie des Sowjetregimes</u>, aus dem Franzosischen ubers. von Harald Hahmann, Frankfurt am Main, FRG: 1966, pp. 153.

Chapter XV, "The Soviet Services", expounds a theory of the possible future growth of KGB power, despite the shackling of the service by the Party apparatchiks after 1953. Garder's predictions were in large measure realized during Brezhnev's tenure and since 1967.

230. GARLINSKI, Josef

THE SWISS CORRIDOR: ESPIONAGE NETWORKS IN SWITZERLAND DURING WORLD WAR II

London, England: Dent, 1981, pp. 222.

An elaboration of the doubtful thesis developed in the author's first book, <u>The Emigres' War</u> (New York, New York: Scribners, 1980) that the British fed relevant enigma production to the Soviets via their Swiss GRU network, the Rote Drei headed by Alexander Rode.

231. GEHLEN, Reinhard

THE SERVICE: THE MEMOIRS OF GENERAL REINHARD GEHLEN

translated from the German <u>Der Dienst</u> by David Irving, introduction by George Bailey

New York, New York: World Publishers, 1972, pp. 386.

The controversial memoirs of the man who was head of "Foreign Armies East" during World War II and the leader of the West German Intelligence Service (BND) until 1968.

232. GERSON, Lennard D.

THE SECRET POLICE IN LENIN'S RUSSIA

Philadelphia, Pennsylvania: Temple University Press, 1976, pp. 332.

A reworked version of the author's Ph.D. thesis at George Washington University: "The Shield and the Sword--Felix Dzerzhinskiy and the Establishment of the Soviet Secret Police" (1973). It deals with the origins, evolution, and operational characteristics of Soviet state security in its first half decade. A solid piece of research and exposition.

233. GRAMONT, Sanche de [pseudonym of Ted Morgan]

THE SECRET WAR: THE STORY OF INTERNATIONAL ESPIONAGE SINCE WORLD WAR II

New York, New York: Putnam, 1962, pp. 515.

See statement on pp. 519-520 that "systematic distortion of the truth is perhaps the basic weakness of Soviet intelligence." Case histories of major espionage incidents 1950-1961. Chapter on "Diplomats, Soldiers, and Espionage" is of special interest.

234. HAZAN, Barukh A.

SOVIET PROPAGANDA: A CASE STUDY OF THE MIDDLE EAST CONFLICT

New York, New York: Wiley, 1976, pp. 293.

See discussion of the KGB's role in the organization and timing of propaganda and disinformation.

235. ---------

SOVIET IMPREGNATIONAL PROPAGANDA

Ann Arbor, Michigan: Ardis, 1982, pp. 180.

Culture, sport, and art as the continuation of politics by other means, "the concealed cutting edge to soften in foreign countries the educational-intellectual ground for later political intentions" (from the foreword). A useful companion to Shultz and Godson's Dezinformatsia: Active Measures in Soviet Strategy (q.v.) and Golitsyn's New Lies for Old (q.v.).

236. HEIJENOORT, Jean van

WITH TROTSKY IN EXILE: FROM PRINKIPO TO COYOACAN

Cambridge, Massachusetts: Harvard University Press, 1978, pp. 164.

See p. 117 for Trotsky's description of Jacques Duclos as an "old GPU agent".

237. HEILBRUNN, Otto

THE SOVIET SECRET SERVICES

U.S. Edition: New York, New York: Praeger, 1956, pp. 216.

U.K. Edition: London, England: Allen and Unwin, 1956, pp. 216.

An account of Soviet Security Service activities during World War II, with emphasis on partisan operations support.

238. HENZE, Paul

THE PLOT TO KILL THE POPE

New York, New York: Scribners, 1984, pp. 216.

Adduces a strong case, based on the available evidence and KGB operational traditions, for Bulgarian/Soviet involvement in the May 1981 attempted assassination of Pope John Paul II.

239. HERMAN, Victor

COMING OUT OF THE ICE: AN UNEXPECTED LIFE

New York, New York: Harcourt, Brace, Jovanovich, 1979, pp. 369.

This powerful memoir is by a recent American returnee from the USSR who went there in the 1930s, and saw the Gulag: "I hope to meet the (American) President...he and his advisers just don't understand the Russian mentality."

240. HINGLEY, Ronald

THE RUSSIAN SECRET POLICE: MUSCOVITE, IMPERIAL RUSSIAN, AND SOVIET POLITICAL SECURITY OPERATIONS, 1565-1970

U.S. Edition: New York, New York: Simon & Schuster, 1971, pp. 313.

U.K. Edition: London, England: Hutchinson, 1970, pp. 305.

The author makes a historical survey of Russian and Soviet intelligence and security activities from Ivan the Terrible to Brezhnev in 1970. It is generally reliable and is one of the few works available covering such a broad time frame.

241. ---------

THE RUSSIAN MIND

U.S. Edition: New York, New York: Charles Scribner Sons, 1972, pp. 307.

U.K. Edition: London, England: Bodley Head, 1978, pp. 247.

Chapter 2, "Communication Systems", provides an unusual treatment of deception and disinformation.

242. HINKLE, Warren

AN ESSENTIAL MEMOIR OF A LUNATIC DECADE

New York, New York: Putnam, 1974, pp. 370.

Hinkle, as a publisher-editor of Ramparts, sponsored a
cold approach to the Soviet Embassy in Mexico City for
information on the Kennedy assassin, Lee Harvey Oswald.
The response was a manuscript defaming the United
States, published in Europe as Amerique Brule (America
Burns) and in Canada as Farewell America.

243. HOHNE, Heinz

CODEWORD: DIREKTOR: THE STORY OF THE RED
ORCHESTRA

translated from the German Kenwort: Direktor by
Richard Barry

U.S. Edition: New York, New York: Coward, McCann,
and Geoghegan, 1971, pp. 310.

Reissued by Ballantine Books, New York, New York:
1982, pp. 370.

U.K. Edition: London, England: Secker and Warburg,
1971, pp. 310.

The author contends that Germans, Russians and others
have overstated the impact of this Soviet network on
the course of World War II.

244. HOLLANDER, Paul

POLITICAL PILGRIMS: TRAVELS OF WESTERN
INTELLECTUALS TO THE SOVIET UNION, CHINA,
AND CUBA

New York, New York: Harper Colophon Books, 1981,
pp. 526.

Hollander's study is a trenchant examination of the
compelling and persistent attraction that twentieth
century leftist police states hold for credulous
Western intellectuals.

245. HOOD, William

MOLE

New York, New York: W.W. Norton & Co., 1982, pp. 317.

Reissued by Ballantine Books, New York, New York: 1983, pp. 320.

Lt. Col. Pyotr Popov, a GRU officer, was probably among the first well-placed agents recruited by the CIA within Soviet Intelligence. He is said to have remained in place from 1952 until exposed by the KGB in 1958. This reconstruction of the case, beginning with Popov's recruitment, is presented by a retired CIA officer.

246. HURT, Henry

SHADRIN: THE SPY WHO NEVER CAME BACK

New York, New York: Reader's Digest Press, 1981, pp. 301.

A sympathetic and poignant account of the disappearance, under mysterious circumstances, of a US citizen and former Soviet Naval officer (Nicholas Artamonov Shadrin) in Vienna in 1975. The author notes that Shadrin, a US government employee, had been serving as double-agent against the KGB.

247. JAKOBSON, Max

THE DIPLOMACY OF THE WINTER WAR: AN ACCOUNT OF THE RUSSO-FINNISH WAR, 1939-1940

Cambridge, Massachusetts: Harvard University Press, 1961, pp. 281.

See pp. 19-93 for the origin and development by the NKVD of an independent channel to the Finnish Foreign Minister, 14 April 1938, via the Soviet 2nd Secretary in Helsinki, Boris Yartsev, and conducted by him explicitly without the knowledge of the Soviet Ambassador in Helsinki, Derevianski. Yartsev was identified by the Helsinki police as an NKVD officer.

248. KAHN, David

THE CODEBREAKERS: THE STORY OF SECRET WRITING

U.S. Edition: New York, New York: MacMillan, 1967, pp. 1164.

U.K. Edition: London, England: Weidenfeld and Nicolson, 1967, pp. 1164.

Abridged U.K. Edition: London, England: Weidenfeld and Nicolson, 1974, pp. 576.

Chapter XVIII, "Russkaya Kriptologia", is one of the few presentations in the open literature about Tsarist and Soviet organization, methodologies, and cases, legal and illegal, in code and cipher matters.

249. --------

HITLER'S SPIES: GERMAN MILITARY INTELLIGENCE IN WORLD WAR II

New York, New York: MacMillan, 1978, pp. 671.

Coverage of Soviet-related operations is scattered throughout; however, see Chapter 18 for the Turkul-Klatt/Max Soviet deception operation against Germany, and Chapters 23 and 24 for other specifics.

250. KETTLE, Michael

SIDNEY REILLY: THE TRUE STORY

London, England: Corgi Books, 1983, pp. 144.

Important because this version of Reilly's origins and family (though not his name, "Rosenbloom") is impossible to square with the version popularized by Robin Bruce Lockhart, Ace of Spies (New York: Stein & Day, 1967). The tangle of fact, hearsay, fancy and disinformation about this British agent who failed in his critical political action operation in Moscow in 1918, and was lured back into the Soviet Union by the OGPU and presumably executed, cries out for dispassionate review, investigation, and re-assessment.

251. KIRKPATRICK, Lyman B., Jr. and Howland
H. SARGEANT

**SOVIET POLITICAL WARFARE TECHNIQUES: ESPIONAGE AND
PROPAGANDA IN THE 1970s**

New York, New York: National Strategy Information
Center, 1972, pp. 82.

Espionage and propaganda are treated separately in this
short monograph on Soviet political warfare. Kirkpatrick's contribution on Soviet espionage is a basic
introductory survey of the organization and selected
operations of the Soviet Secret Services. Several short
case studies highlight Soviet intelligence cases since
the 1917 Revolution.

252. KUCHEROV, Samuel

**ORGANS OF SOVIET ADMINISTRATION OF JUSTICE, THEIR
HISTORY AND OPERATION**

Leiden, Netherlands: E.J. Brill, 1970, pp. 754.

See pp. 55-77, "The All-Russian Extraordinary Com-
mission (VeCheka)", pp. 71-77, "The State Political
Administration-GPU", pp. 661-715, "Revolution and
Socialist Legality", and "Conclusions."

253. LEE, Andrea

RUSSIAN JOURNAL

1st U.S. Edition: New York, New York: Random
House, 1981, pp. 239.

2nd U.S. Edition: New York, New York: Vintage
Books, 1984, pp. 239.

Brightly written observations on life from the youthful
graduate student perspective at Moscow State University, Leningrad and elsewhere in the Soviet Union,
including the informant and surveillance system. See
pp. 112-123 for an evocative encounter with Victor
Louis.

254. LEGGETT, George H.

THE CHEKA: LENIN'S POLITICAL POLICE: THE ALL-RUSSIAN EXTRAORDINARY COMMISSION FOR COMBATING COUNTER-REVOLUTION AND SABOTAGE, DECEMBER 1917 TO FEBRUARY 1922

Oxford, England: Oxford University Press, 1981, pp. 514.

Exceptionally well-researched, balanced and informative, this book is a treasure of documentation and insight on the early years of both State Security and Lenin's Party-State.

255. LEHOVICH, Dimitry V.

WHITE AGAINST RED: THE LIFE OF GENERAL ANTON DENIKIN

New York, New York: Norton, 1974, pp. 556.

Biography based on Denikin's papers at Columbia University, New York City. Two chapters are of importance for Denikin's views of the intelligence and security aspects of the "Trust" operation, developed from Moscow, 1921-1927, and successor operations, including the kidnappings of Kutyepov (1930) and General Miller (1937).

256. LEITES, Nathan Constantin

A STUDY OF BOLSHEVISM

Glencoe, Illinois: Free Press, 1953, pp. 639.

See Chapter XIII: "Deception", "The Danger of Being Deceived", "The Defense Against Being Deceived", and "How Far Can the Enemy be Deceived ?" (pp. 324-340).

257. LEVINE, Isaac Don

EYEWITNESS TO HISTORY: MEMOIRS AND REFLECTIONS OF A FOREIGN CORRESPONDENT FOR HALF A CENTURY

New York, New York: Hawthorn Books, 1973, pp. 305.

Important recollections of a journalist eyewitness and, at times, participant in developments affecting the Soviet Security Service since the Revolution. Among them: Krivitsky in the US and his death, the Trotsky assassination, and the execution of the Romanovs.

258. LEVYTSKY, Boris

THE USES OF TERROR: THE SOVIET SECRET POLICE 1917-1970

translated by H.A. Piehler

U.S. Edition: New York, New York: Coward, McCann and Geoghegen, 1972, pp. 349.

U.K. Edition: London, England: Sidgwick and Jackson, 1971, pp. 349.

German Edition: Die Rote Inquisition. Frankfurt, FRG: Frankfurter Societats - Druckerei GmbH, 1967, pp. 395.

French Edition: Inquisition Rouge. Paris, France: Editions Robert Laffont, 1969.

Badly translated from the German edition, Die Rote Inquisition, which in turn was a re-working and re-interpretation of the author's Vom Roten Terror Zur Sozialistishen Gesetzlichkeit: Der Sowyetishche Sicherheitsdienst (From Red Terror to Socialist Legality. The Soviet Secret Service). Munich, FRG: 1961, pp. 302. Should be used with caution.

259. LIGUE DE LA LIBERTE

SOVIET SPIES IN THE SCIENTIFIC AND TECHNICAL FIELDS

Belgium: Ligue de la Liberte, Centre d'information et de Documentation, January 1968, pp. 96.

A review, with photographs covering the activity of 36 Soviet Scientific and Technical officers in 7 countries: Australia, Canada, Netherlands, New Zealand, Sweden, US, and UK.

260. LINDSEY, Robert

THE FALCON AND THE SNOWMAN: A TRUE STORY OF FRIENDSHIP AND ESPIONAGE

New York, New York: Simon & Schuster, 1979, pp. 359.

A detailed treatment of the case of Andrew Daulton Lee and Christopher John Boyce, convicted in 1977 in the TRW, KH-11 satellite case.

261. MARTIN, David C.

WILDERNESS OF MIRRORS

New York, New York: Harper & Row, 1980, pp. 236.

Reissued by Ballantine Books, New York, New York: 1982, pp. 233.

A journalist's account which claims to plumb the Counterintelligence/Counterespionage wars between the KGB and the CIA. Martin focuses on the careers of two major figures in post-war US intelligence, William K. Harvey and James J. Angleton. An important work because it contains unique, albeit selective and incomplete information on major Soviet and Warsaw Pact defectors and the controversies they generated in the United States and certain Allied countries regarding Soviet penetrations [e.g., Goleniewski, Golitsyn and Nosenko]. Martin's interpretations of events, the alleged flaws in his account, and his observations on the personalities involved, provoked much debate. See: Edward J. Epstein's review in The New York Times Book Review, 18 May 1980, and David Martin's response with Epstein's reply, The New York Times Book Review, 6 July 1980; Scott Burke, "If Treason Prosper", Policy Review, Fall 1980, pp. 163-167; Andrew Boyle, "The CIA's Search for the Super Mole", The Washington Post Bookworld, 18 May 1980. See also, the evaluative annotation in George C. Constantinides, Intelligence and Espionage: An Analytical Bibliography (q.v.).

262. MATTHEWS, Mervyn

PRIVILEGE IN THE SOVIET UNION: A CASE STUDY OF ELITE LIFE-STYLES UNDER COMMUNISM

London, England: Allen & Unwin, 1978, pp. 197.

Relates the security and intelligence services to the elitism of political, economic and social privileges fixed by Soviet law and administrative practice.

263. MAUNY, Erik de

RUSSIAN PROSPECT: NOTES OF A MOSCOW CORRESPONDENT

U.S. Edition: New York, New York: Atheneum, 1970, pp. 320.

U.K. Edition: London, England: Macmillan, 1969, pp. 320.

This incisive commentary by a former BBC correspondent in Moscow relates details of a meeting, not elsewhere reported, with the British defector Philby, in 1965. See Chapter IX, "A Meeting At The Moskva" (pp. 187-215).

264. MEAD, Margaret

SOVIET ATTITUDES TOWARD AUTHORITY: AN INTERDISCIPLINARY APPROACH TO PROBLEMS OF SOVIET CHARACTER

Westport, Connecticut: Greenwood Press, 1979, pp. 148; reprint of the 1951 edition.

Chapter XI, "The Place of the Political Police in the Soviet Authority System", is of particular interest to those studying the Soviet security and intelligence services.

265. MEYER, Alfred G.

THE SOVIET POLITICAL SYSTEM: AN INTERPRETATION

New York, New York: Random House, 1965, pp. 494.

See Chapter XIX for a discussion of the use of terror as a means of crushing dissent.

266. MEYER, Cord

FACING REALITY: FROM WORLD FEDERALISM TO THE CIA

1st U.S. Edition: New York, New York: Harper & Row, 1980, pp. 433.

2nd U.S. Edition: Washington, D.C.: University Press of America, 1982, pp. 433.

In 1951, the author joined the CIA where he served for more than 25 years. One of his assignments was as head of the CIA's International Organizations Division which was charged with countering the Soviet political and propaganda offensive against the Free World. Chapters on the Cold War and on the US-controlled Radio Free Europe and Radio Liberty are particularly illuminating, as are the chapters on the Soviet Union and the KGB. See Chapter XIII, "The Soviet 'Apparat'-Government" (pp. 285-311) and Chapter XIV, "The Soviet 'Apparat'-KGB" (pp. 312-330).

267. MONAS, Sidney

THE THIRD SECTION: POLICE AND SOCIETY IN RUSSIA UNDER NICHOLAS I

Cambridge, Massachusetts: Harvard University Press, 1961, pp. 354.

An excellent study of the period in Russian history which witnessed the institutionalization of the secret police. Dr. Monas not only discusses the inception and operations of the Third Section, but also analyzes the impact that organization had on 19th century Russian society.

268. MURPHY, Paul J.

BREZHNEV, SOVIET POLITICIAN

Jefferson, North Carolina: McFarland & Co., 1981, pp. 363.

Useful open-source biography does not lose sight of the KGB's role and mission in Brezhnev's rise to power and tenure.

269. MURRAY, John

A SPY CALLED SWALLOW: THE TRUE STORY OF NORA, THE RUSSIAN AGENT

London, England: W.H. Allen, 1978, pp. 175.

A happy sequel to the bitter-sweet story of the daughter of a prestigious security service official, purged from her liaison position with the Soviet Foreign Office in 1938, who became an informant in 1941 and targetted on an official of the British Embassy, Moscow. See, Nora Murray [Korzhenko], I Spied for Stalin (New York: Wilfrid, Funk, Inc., 1951, pp. 256).

270. MYKLEBUST, Svein Lorents

THE GREATEST DECEPTION IN THE HISTORY OF WARFARE: HITLER'S DECEPTIVE OPERATIONS IN THE MONTHS PRIOR TO THE ATTACK ON RUSSIA IN JUNE 1941

Madison, Wisconsin: University of Wisconsin, Dissertation No. 8015221, 1980, pp. 315.

271. NEWMAN, Joseph, ed.

FAMOUS SOVIET SPIES: THE KREMLIN'S SECRET WEAPON

Washington, D.C.: Books by U.S. News and World Report, 1973, pp. 223.

This short treatment of KGB and GRU organization presents case histories previously published elsewhere.

272. NIEMEYER, Gerhart

AN INQUIRY INTO SOVIET MENTALITY

with the assistance of John S. Reshetar, Jr.

New York, New York: Praeger, 1956, pp. 113.

See pp. 59-63: "Soviet Economic and Military Intelligence."

273. OSADCHY, Mikhaylo

CATARACT

translated from the Ukrainian <u>Bilmo</u>. Edited and annotated by Marco Carynnyk

U.S. Edition: New York, New York: Harcourt, Brace, Jovanovich, 1976, pp. 240.

French Edition:<u>Cataracte</u>, traduit de L'Ukrainien par Kalena Uhryn, Paris, France: Fayard, 1974, pp. 332.

See discussion of General V.V. Fedorchuk's succession to V.F. Nikitchenko as KGB Chairman in the Ukraine.

274. PAGE, Bruce, David LEITCH and Phillip KNIGHTLEY

THE PHILBY CONSPIRACY

1st U.S. Edition: Garden City, New York: Doubleday, 1968, pp. 300.

2nd U.S. Edition: with an introduction by John Le Carre, New York, New York: New American Library, 1969, pp. 278.

Reissued by Ballantine Books, New York, New York: 1981, pp. 295.

1st U.K. Edition: <u>Philby: The Spy Who Betrayed a Generation</u>, with an introduction by John Le Carre, Harmondsworth, New York, New York: Penguin, 1969, pp. 336.

2nd U.K. Edition: <u>Philby: The Spy Who Betrayed a Generation</u>, with an introduction by John Le Carre, London, England: Sphere, 1977, pp. 336.

A team of journalists detail the Philby Affair, including Philby's lengthy service as a Soviet agent, his rise to senior ranks within the British Intelligence Service, his relationships with the defectors Burgess and Maclean, and Philby's tour in the US in an intelligence liaison capacity.

275. PERRAULT, Giles

THE RED ORCHESTRA

U.S. Edition: translated from the French by Peter Wiles and Len Ortzen, New York, New York: Simon & Schuster, 1969, pp. 512.

U.K. Edition: translated from the French by Peter Wiles and Len Ortzen, London, England: Barker, 1968, pp. 496.

French Edition: L'Orchestra Rouge, Paris, France: Libraire Artheme Fayard, 1967.

An account of the Rote Kapelle, the network that provided the Soviets with important military and political intelligence prior to and during World War II.

276. PETHYBRIDGE, Roger

A KEY TO SOVIET POLITICS: THE CRISIS OF THE 'ANTI PARTY' GROUP

London, England: Allen & Unwin, 1962, pp. 207.

An early and significant contribution to the theory of security service "down grading" under Khrushchev.

277. PILAT, Oliver Ramsay

THE ATOM SPIES

New York, New York: Putnam, 1952, pp. 312.

One of several available accounts of the Soviet atomic espionage rings operating in the US during the 1940s and 1950s.

278. PINCHER, Chapman

THEIR TRADE IS TREACHERY

London, England: Sidgwick and Jackson, 1981, pp. 240.

A sensational expose by a British journalist of high
level penetrations of MI5, MI6, and the Foreign Office
by the KGB and other communist services. The author
apparently acquired some sensitive information which
led to his wide-ranging suggestions of treason. Though
some maintain that he is careless with data, Pincher
sheds light on such past activities as Soviet strategic
deception operations during World War II (the Klatt-
Turkul connection) and KGB defector Golitsyn's revelations about Khrushchev's and Shelepin's re-orientation
of KGB policy towards greater "active measures" in the
late 1950s and early 1960s.

Despite defects this is an important work of disclosure
and expose regarding the long-range penetration of the
British.

279. --------

TOO SECRET TOO LONG

U.S. Edition: New York, New York: St. Martin's
Press, 1984, pp. 638.

U.K. Edition: London, England: Sidgwick &
Jackson, Ltd., 1984, pp. 638.

A much more detailed follow-on, in the same vein as
Their Trade is Treachery (q.v.). Drawing openly on the
revelations of former British intelligence and security
officers, Pincher makes a massive effort to demonstrate
that a former chief of MI5, Sir Roger Hollis, was a
Soviet "mole" responsible for an alarming number of
Soviet intelligence coups and concomitant British and
Allied security scandals. Pincher's evidence is
incomplete and fractious; a storm of controversy
preceeded and accompanied the book's publication.
Notwithstanding the controversy, the work surfaces
numerous operations, cases and details thereof never
before or rarely aired in published literature (e.g.
Hollis' contacts during his China sojourn; the GRU
activities of several members of the Kuczynski family
before, during and after World War II; the post-war
analysis of intercepted coded Soviet radio traffic from
World War II, called Operation Bride/Venona, which led
to several breakthroughs in Soviet espionage cases).
This work could prove to be a major point of departure
as a road map for the examination of a plethora of
interconnected Soviet intelligence cases spanning a
half century.

280. PIPES, Richard

RUSSIA UNDER THE OLD REGIME

U.S. Edition: New York, New York: Scribner, 1974, pp. 360.

U.K. Editon: London, England: Wiedinfeld & Nicolson, 1974, pp. 360.

Chapter XI, "Towards the Police State", is an interpretation of the development of security functions which bridges the periods of the Tsar and Kommissar.

281. READ, Anthony and David FISHER

OPERATION LUCY, MOST SECRET SPY RING OF THE SECOND WORLD WAR

New York, New York: Coward, McCann & Geoghegan, 1981, pp. 257.

Sustains the dubious thesis that the Roessler and other Rado material was fed to the Soviets by radio from Switzerland at the direct insistence and oversight of Churchill. Fuses the Enigma revelations with the Foote-Guisan-Rado materials and asserts that Foote and "Sissy" (Rachael Dubendorfer) were British-controlled agents. No footnotes or source citations.

282. RHOER, Edward van der

MASTER SPY: A TRUE STORY OF ALLIED ESPIONAGE IN BOLSHEVIK RUSSIA

New York, New York: Scribners, 1981, pp. 260.

This re-evocation of British and Allied operations in Russia after the Revolution focuses on the life and death of the British agent (of Russian origin) Sidney Reilly. Reilly's extraordinary performance and his ultimate sacrifice are recounted together with the questionable theory that he was actually a Soviet double agent.

283. ROMERSTEIN, Herbert

SOVIET SUPPORT FOR INTERNATIONAL TERRORISM

Washington, D.C.: The Foundation for Democratic Education, Inc., 1981, pp. 44.

A useful account of the ideological underpinnings and modus operandi of international terrorism and its linkage to the Soviets.

284. ROSENFELDT, Neils Erik

KNOWLEDGE AND POWER: THE ROLE OF STALIN'S SECRET CHANCELLERY IN THE SOVIET SYSTEM OF GOVERNMENT

Copenhagen, Denmark: Copenhagen University Institute of Slavonic Studies, No. 5, Rosenkilde and Bagger, 1978, pp. 219.

A valuable monograph on the organization and development of Stalin's "osobyi' sektor" (secret sector or department) which served as a powerful instrument of his personal control over Party and State organs, in particular, the Security and Intelligence services.

285. ROSITZKE, Harry

THE KGB: THE EYES OF RUSSIA

Garden City, New York: Doubleday, 1981, pp. 295.

A general, introductory and anecdotal account of the subject by a former CIA officer. Its lack of documentation and some debatable assertations, [the KGB] "is a straightforward, secret service, even in its more devious and deceptive practices" (p.ix), or "organized ethnic and religious minorities face the KGB with the least problem of security and control" (p. 254), limit the utility of this work.

286. SALISBURY, Harrison Evans

WITHOUT FEAR OR FAVOR: THE NEW YORK TIMES AND ITS TIMES

New York, New York: New York Times Books, 1980, pp. 630.

See p. 462 for a discussion of the charge, made in 1979, that Walter Duranty, New York Times correspondent in the Soviet Union during the 1920s and 1930s, was a Soviet agent.

287. SAWATSKY, John

MEN IN THE SHADOWS: THE RCMP SECURITY SERVICE

New York, New York: Doubleday, 1980, pp. 302.

Contains much useful information on KGB personnel, methods and operations in Canada, and RCMP counter-measures. The Gouzenko defection is recapitulated and re-assessed at pp. 72-90. Officers under diplomatic cover for espionage activities in Canada from 1956-1979 are listed on pp. 289-293. The text includes a hard-sell statement of the case for the separation of the RCMP from the security and counterintelligence-mission.

288. SAYERS, Michael and Albert E. KAHN

THE GREAT CONSPIRACY: THE SECRET WAR AGAINST SOVIET RUSSIA

Boston, Massachusetts: Little, Brown and Co., 1946, pp. 433.

This is a pro-Soviet slant on the "Trust" (Trest) case and other operations of the Soviet service. Promoted by the CPUSA, Soviet sponsorship of this book was identified in Congressional testimony in 1952 by Igor Bogolepov, a former Soviet official who claimed to have seen the original Russian manuscript at the Foreign Ministry in Moscow before it was sent to New York City.

See and compare: Committee on the Judiciary, United States Senate, Subcommittee to Investigate the Administration of the Internal Security Act and Other Internal Security Laws, Institute of Pacific Relations, Part 13. Testimony of Igor Bogolepov, 82nd Congress, 2nd Session, 1952, (Washington, D.C., GPO), pp. 4513-4514.

289. SCOTT, William F. and Harriet Fast SCOTT

THE SOVIET CONTROL STRUCTURE: CAPABILITIES FOR WARTIME SURVIVAL

New York, New York: Crane, Russak for the National Strategy Information Center, 1983, pp. 146.

See "Role of the KGB and MVD" (pp. 10-12) and "KGB and MVD Control Capabilities" (pp. 97-104, 104-111).

290. SEALE, Patrick and Maureen McCONVILLE

THE LONG ROAD TO MOSCOW

1st U.S. Edition: New York, New York: Simon & Schuster, 1973, pp. 282.

2nd U.S. Edition: New York, New York: Penguin, 1978, pp. 349.

U.K. Edition: London, England: Hamilton, 1973, pp. 282.

One of the better journalistic accounts of the Philby case. It is, however, overtaken by the detail of the case offered in Boyle's The Fourth Man (q.v.) and Pincher's Too Secret Too Long (q.v.).

291. SENN, Alfred Erich

ASSASSINATION IN SWITZERLAND: THE MURDER OF VATSLAV VOROVSKY

Madison, Wisconsin: University of Wisconsin, 1981, pp. 219.

Vorovsky, a Soviet diplomat, was assassinated by Maurice Alexandre Conradi, a Russian with Swiss family ties, at the Lausanne conference, May 10, 1923. This is a thoroughly documented account of the background to the assassination, the investigation of the crime, and the subsequent trial and acquittal of Conradi.

292. SHULTZ, Richard H., Jr. and Roy GODSON

DEZINFORMATSIA: ACTIVE MEASURES IN SOVIET
STRATEGY

New York, New York: Pergammon-Brassey's, 1984, pp.
211.

One of the few recent, authoritative examinations of
the concept, organization and operation of "active
measures" as a critical contemporary element of Soviet
political strategy. In addition to thematic analysis,
coverage includes one of the few public elucidations of
the Pathe case in France, and interviews with Czech and
Soviet practitioners of this proven Soviet art form.

293. SMITH, Thomas B.

THE OTHER ESTABLISHMENT: AN IN-DEPTH STUDY OF WHAT
INDIVIDUAL LIFE IS REALLY LIKE IN COMMUNIST-
CONTROLLED COUNTRIES

Chicago, Illinois: Regnery Gateway, 1984, pp.
205.

Although billed as a study of what individual life is
like in Communist-controlled countries, this is more
precisely an elucidation on the web of control documentation issued from the Party-Security-State combine.
The Soviet internal security system is based on the
control of individual identity, activity and movements
through an interlocking set of mandatory personal
documents: the Identity document (Pasport), the
Residence Registration (Propiska), the Work Booklet
(Trudovaya Knizhka), and the Military Reserve Document
(Voyennyy Bilet). This first public study of the system
includes 46 photos of internal passports and other
documents.

294. SNELLING, O.F.

RARE BOOKS AND RARER PEOPLE: SOME PERSONAL
REMINISCENCES OF 'THE TRADE'

London, England: W. Shaw, 1982, pp. 256.

On the Soviet illegals in London in 1961, the Krogers
(who used a book dealer cover) and Lonsdale, see "My
Three Spies" (pp. 204-247).

295. SQUIRE, Peter Stansfield

THE THIRD DEPARTMENT: THE ESTABLISHMENT AND
PRACTICES OF THE POLITICAL POLICE IN THE RUSSIA OF
NICHOLAS I

Cambridge, England: Cambridge University Press,
1968, pp. 272.

Similar to the Monas book, Squire's work provides more
detail on the secret police of Nicholas I. Useful for
contrasting the scope of police authority of pre-
Revolutionary Russia with that of its Soviet successor.

296. STERLING, Claire

THE TERROR NETWORK: THE SECRET WAR OF
INTERNATIONAL TERRORISM

U.S. Edition: New York, New York: Holt, Rinehart
and Winston, 1981, pp. 357.

U.K. Edition: London, England: Weidenfeld and
Nicolson, 1981, pp. 357.

Sterling's work stirred international controversy
because of her linkage of Soviet/East European security
services to various worldwide terrorist organizations
and operations.

297. --------

THE TIME OF THE ASSASSINS: ANATOMY OF AN
INVESTIGATION

New York, New York: Holt, Rinehart and Winston,
1984, pp. 264.

Like Henze's The Plot to Kill the Pope (q.v.), Sterling's book draws the same conclusions as to Bulgarian-
Soviet complicity in the attempted assassination of
John Paul II. Half her book, however, delves into what
she sees as the hesitancy and incredulity of Western
governments when faced with the evidence and implications of the failed assassination.

298. TANNER, Vaino

THE WINTER WAR: FINLAND AGAINST RUSSIA 1939-1940

Stanford, California: Stanford University Press, 1957, pp. 274.

On secret NKVD backchannel diplomatic negotiations (the Yartsev negotiations) in Finland, April-December 1938, followed up by another Soviet secret intermediary (see pp. 3-21). See also entry #247.

299. TAUBMAN, William

THE VIEW FROM LENIN HILLS: SOVIET YOUTH IN FERMENT

U.S. Edition: New York, New York: Coward-McCann, 1967, pp. 249.

U.K. Edition: London, England: H. Hamilton, 1968, pp. 249.

A candid and probably optimistic memoir by an American exchange student at Moscow State University, 1965-1966. See Chapter IX, "Me and My Shadows" (pp. 96-108) for details of surveillance at the University and for comments on the system outside the capital (pp. 222-223).

300. THEBERGE, James D.

THE SOVIET PRESENCE IN LATIN AMERICA

New York, New York: Crane, Russak for the National Strategy Information Center, 1974, pp. 107.

See Chapter IV, "Soviet Espionage and Subversion" (pp. 26-36) and Chapter V, "Moscow's Support for Revolutionary Violence" (pp. 37-46).

301. --------, ed.

RUSSIA IN THE CARIBBEAN

Washington, D.C.: Center for Strategic and International Studies, 1973, pp. 166, 2 volumes.

114

Volume I is the work of several panelists. Volume II is
comment by Theberge. See especially Chapter VII,
"Soviet Espionage and Political Subversion...Moscow's
Cuban Base, Moscow's Mexican Base" (pp. 43-52).

302. TOLSTOY, Nikolai

STALIN'S SECRET WAR

U.S. Edition: New York, New York: Holt, Rinehart
and Winston, 1981, pp. 463.

U.K. Edition: London, England: J. Cape, 1981, pp.
463.

The grand-nephew of Leo Tolstoy chronicles and inter-
prets Stalin's savaging of his people. For example, the
slaughter of the Polish officers at Katyn and other
sites was intended to forestall a potential uprising in
the Western USSR by killing off the potential leadership.

303. TREVOR-ROPER, Hugh Redwald

THE PHILBY AFFAIR: ESPIONAGE, TREASON AND SECRET
SERVICES

London, England: Kimber, 1968, pp. 126.

The Philby case is critically examined by a distinguished British historian who was also a member of MI5
during World War II.

304. VILLEMAREST, Pierre F. de

L'ESPIONAGE SOVIETIQUE EN FRANCE (1944-1969)

Paris, France: Nouvelle Editon Latine, 1969, pp.
316.

The most knowledgeable and comprehensive treatment of
Soviet operations in France for the period noted.

305. VERIDICUS [pseudonym of Henri Guilbeaux]

SUISSE ET SOVIETS: HISTOIRE D'UN CONFLIT:
L'EXPULSION DE LA MISSION SOVIETIQUE, L'ASSASSINAT
IMPUNI DE VOROVSKY, POUR-QUOI L'URSS N'ASSISTAIT
PAS A LA CONFERANCE DU DISARMEMENT

[Switzerland and the Soviets: Story of a Conflict:
The Expulsion of the Soviet Mission, The Un-
punished Assassination of Vorovsky, Why the USSR
did not Help at the Disarmament Conference]

preface de Mathias Morhardt

Paris, France: A. Delpeuch, 1926, pp. 171.

An early Soviet "influence" operation. This un-
abashedly pro-Soviet publication presumably was written
to specification in order to back the Soviets in the
discussions that followed the Vorovsky assassination.
There were extensive Soviet efforts to place copies of
this work in libraries in Switzerland and in other
countries.

306. WALKIN, Jakob

THE RISE OF DEMOCRACY IN PRE-REVOLUTIONARY RUSSIA:
POLITICAL AND SOCIAL INSTITUTIONS UNDER THE LAST
THREE TSARS

New York, New York: Praeger, 1962, pp. 320.

See Chapter III, "The Police State--Tsarist Version"
(pp. 41-72).

307. WAXMONSKY, Gary Richard

POLICE AND POLITICS IN SOVIET SOCIETY, 1921-1929

Princeton, New Jersey: Princeton University, Ph.D.
Dissertation No. DA.8216296, 1982, pp. 394.

The author suggests that the "hypertrophy of the
political police" by the end of the 1920s was more the
product of "sub-cosmic" factors, such as "contradictory
party leadership demands" or "the default of contiguous

Party and State hierarchies", than the inevitable
by-products of a "coercive political order." On this
conclusion, compare with Leggett's The Cheka: Lenin's
Political Police (q.v.) and Gerson's The Secret Police
in Lenin's Russia (q.v.).

308. WEINSTEIN, Allen

PERJURY: THE HISS-CHAMBERS CASE

New York, New York: Alfred A. Knopf, 1978, pp.
674.

This carefully documented study finds for Chambers.
Having identified and interviewed the wife of Chambers'
Soviet handler as a recent emigrant from the USSR to
Israel, Weinstein was able to provide another of the
missing links in the Sorge case--the identification of
Sorge's original GRU superior, "Alex", in Shanghai
(1929-1930) as Alexander Ulanovskiy, a well-known GRU
illegal in the US and Denmark in the thirties.

309. WEST, Nigel [pseudonym]

MI5: BRITISH SECURITY OPERATIONS 1909-1945

U.K. Edition: London, England: Bodley Head, 1981,
pp. 365.

U.S. Edition: New York, New York: Stein & Day,
1982, pp. 365.

In this straightforward but uneven history of MI5, the
British Security Service, most attention is devoted to
MI5 operations against German activities. See Chapter
II for coverage on Soviet intelligence operations in
the inter-war period, especially the circumstances of
the 1927 ARCOS raid.

The Postscript addresses briefly the Blunt case and the
controversy raised by Pincher's Their Trade is Treachery (q.v.).

310. --------

THE CIRCUS: MI5 OPERATIONS 1945-1972

New York, New York: Stein & Day, 1983, pp. 196.

Controversial expose of Soviet operations against British and American targets; compare with Chapman Pincher (q.v.).

311. WEST, Rebecca

THE NEW MEANING OF TREASON

New York, New York: Viking Press, 1962, pp. 374.

An updated and revised version of Dame Rebecca West's The Meaning of Treason. Her accounts of the psychology and motivations of celebrated British spies, traitors, and defectors include the cases of William Joyce, John Amery, Dr. Alan Nunn May, Dr. Klaus Fuchs, Bruno Pontecorvo, Donald Maclean, Guy Burgess, and George Blake.

312. WHALEY, Barton

CODEWORD BARBAROSSA

Cambridge, Massachusetts: MIT Press, 1973, pp. 376.

An analysis of the 1941 German invasion of the Soviet Union with several interesting features: an elaboration of the Wohlstetter concept of "signals" and "noise" in the field of warning intelligence; a look at pre-World War II intelligence operations, especially in the area of communications intelligence; and a new interpretation of the Soviet view of pre-war German offensive preparations. The work seems to attribute more success to German deception than is warranted by the evidence.

313. WHITESIDE, Thomas

AN AGENT IN PLACE: THE WENNERSTROM AFFAIR

London, England: Heinemann, 1967, pp. 150.

Reissued by Ballantine Books, New York, New York: 1983, pp. 160.

Colonel Stig Eric Wennerstrom, a Swedish Air Force officer, provided Swedish and US/NATO military secrets to the Soviets for fifteen years. He had served in Washington as an air attache. In 1964, he received a life sentence.

314. WHITTLIN, Thaddeus

   COMMISSAR: THE LIFE AND DEATH OF LAVRENTY PAVLOVICH BERIA

   New York, New York: MacMillan, 1972, pp. 566.

An anecdotal treatment of Beria's activities from his pre-revolutionary activities to his death in 1953 (with claims that both Beria and Stalin were Okhrana agents). Unsourced assertations and apparent hearsay evidence limit its reliability (e.g., detailed alleged conversations between Beria and other Soviet officials are reconstructed for the reader).

315. WOLFE, Bertram D.

   A LIFE IN TWO CENTURIES: AN AUTOBIOGRAPHY

   with an introduction by Leonard Schapiro

   New York, New York: Stein & Day, 1981, pp. 728.

Posthumous memoir by a founding member of the CPUSA who became one of the most literate and effective critics of Communism and the Soviet Union.

316. WOLIN, Simon and Robert M. SLUSSER, eds.

   THE SOVIET SECRET POLICE

   Westport, Connecticut: Greenwood Press, 1974, pp. 408.

A foundation work on the Soviet Intelligence and Security Services, essential to the further study of the subject. Wolin and Slusser had intended that it serve as a point of departure for studies of the subject in greater depth and breadth.

317. X., Mr., with Bruce E. HENDERSON and   C.C. CYR

DOUBLE EAGLE: THE AUTOBIOGRAPHY OF A POLISH SPY
WHO DEFECTED TO THE WEST

Indianapolis, Indiana: Bobbs-Merrill Co., 1979,
pp. 227.

Reissued by Ballantine Books with new material
especially prepared for this edition, New York,
New York: 1982, pp. 277.

A somewhat troublesome work by a former Polish Security
Service (UB) Lt. Col., who defected to the US after
having worked in place in Norway (1964-1967) where he
was recruited.   It is one of the few writings since
Monat's Spy in the U.S. (q.v.) to provide a window on
the Soviet advisory system in Bloc services.

318. YANOV, Alexander

THE ORIGINS OF AUTOCRACY: IVAN THE TERRIBLE IN
RUSSIAN HISTORY

translated by Stephen Dunn

Berkeley, California: University of California
Press, 1981, pp. 339.

An important, recent re-interpretation of the "Oprichnina" and other aspects of the authoritarian tradition.

319. ZILE, Zigurds L.; Robert SHARLET; and Jean C.
LOVE

THE SOVIET LEGAL SYSTEM AND ARMS INSPECTION: A
CASE STUDY IN POLICY IMPLEMENTATION

New York, New York: Praeger, 1972, pp. 394.

The KGB organizational breakdown (pp. 232-233) is now
obsolete. Otherwise, this is a diligent and illuminating study, based on open materials in Russian and
in English. It probes the possible and probable
relationships of the Soviet Security Service, among
other elements of government in the Soviet Union, to
specific US operational and policy interests.

Articles and Chapters

320.

"ACTS OF THE APOSTLES"

Observer (London), 8 November 1981, p. 25.

Details and ruminations on the Soviet infiltration of
Cambridge University, 1933-1945. Adds to information
previously published in Pincher's Their Trade is
Treachery (q.v.).

321.

**"A CHANGE IN SHIFT FOR THE KGB: SOVIET INTELLI-
GENCE CHANGES PROMPT PAKISTANIS TO WONDER IF
SOMETHING BIG IS ABOUT TO START"**

Far Eastern Economic Review 97 (June 15, 1979):
pp. 2.

Prescient data and analytic resume of the reorganization of the KGB and GRU Residenturas in Karachi
and in Islamabad shortly before the invasion of
Afghanistan. Soviet "legal" organization and personalities are described in detail.

322.

"ESPIONAGE AS AN INSTRUMENT OF COMMUNIST POLICY"

The British Survey (London), no. 136, (July 1960),
pp. 24.

323.

"FROM AZEFF TO AGCA"

Survey 27 (Autumn-Winter 1983): pp. 1-89.

Collection of articles and short pieces dealing with
Russian-Soviet-inspired provocations and assassinations, from pre-Revolutionary Okhrana operations to
the 1981 attempt on Pope John Paul II.

324.

"GREEK FEELERS TO MOSCOW"

The Economist. Foreign Report, 1 March 1978, pp.
7-8.

A commentary on the appointment of Ivan Udaltsov, a
senior KGB officer as Ambassador to Greece. Udaltsov
was Counsellor in Prague, 1968.

325.

"THE KGB"

New York Times, 23 December 1975, pp. 1, 24.

Third article in a series on espionage. Discusses how
the Soviet KGB has developed into the world's largest
and most formidable security and espionage agency, has
prime responsibility for maintaining internal political
control, and Chairman Yuri Andropov has a strong voice
in all policy decisions.

326.

"THE KGB EXPANDS ITS INFLUENCE"

Soviet Analyst 7 (September 28, 1978): pp. 2-3.

Discusses the re-titling of the KGB's administrative
position in the Soviet Government in July 1978, from
"KGB Under the Council of Ministers" to "KGB of the
U.S.S.R."

327.

"THE KGB OFFENSIVE IN WESTERN EUROPE"

The Economist. Foreign Report, 4 February 1976,
pp. 1-3.

328.

"KGB OVERTURES TO BRITISH JEWRY"

The Economist. Foreign Report, 21 September 1977,
pp. 1-2.

Professor Grigoriy Lvovich Bondarenko, head of the
International Department of the Oriental Institute of
the Soviet Academy of Sciences, is described as a
senior KGB officer targetted against the Israelis.

329.

"KGB POSTINGS IN THE MIDDLE EAST"

The Economist. Foreign Report, 8 March 1978, pp.
1-2.

Appointments of A.D. Shelenikov, N.K. Krykunov, and
N.A. Baratov are discussed.

330.

"THE KGB'S UNITED NATIONS BASE"

Soviet Analyst 4 (July 3, 1975): pp. 1-3.

331.

"LIVING IN THE KGB'S SHADOW"

Observer (London), 25 June 1976.

Quoting an un-named Soviet source, this provocative
piece named the KGB Chief as Brezhnev's "favorite
successor" and asked the question "Could Andropov turn
out to be a liberal?".

332.

"THE MEMOIRS OF RETIRED SOVIET POLICE AGENTS"

Radio Liberty Research RL 425/76 (September 29, 1976): pp. 3.

Radio Liberty surveys the continuing Soviet output glorifying the image of the secret and ordinary police, and notes the preparations then in course for the centenary celebration of the birth of Felix Dzerzhinskiy.

333.

"A MOLE AND HIS MASTERS. EXPULSION OF SOVIET SPIES AND THE ARREST OF A MALAY AGENT MARK A TOUGHER MALAYSIAN FOREIGN POLICY"

Far Eastern Economic Review 99 (July 24, 1981): pp. 9.

334.

"OBITUARY OF S. TSVIGUN"

Washington Post, 23 January 1982, p. B10.

335.

"POLITICAL FORGERIES IN LONDON"

The Economist. Foreign Report, 7 September 1977, pp. 1-2.

336.

"PRAISE FOR KGB ON ANNIVERSARY"

Soviet World Outlook 3 (January 15, 1978).

Reviews the celebration of the 100th anniversary of Dzerzhinskiy's birth and the 60th anniversary of the founding of the KGB, citing articles in Kommunist (December 1977), and Pravda (20 December 1977).

337.

"PROBLEMS OF BREZHNEV'S POLICE: #1-THE MVD"

Soviet Analyst 10 (November 18, 1981): pp. 6-7.

338.

"PROBLEMS OF BREZHNEV'S POLICE: #2-THE KGB"

Soviet Analyst 10 (December 16, 1981): pp. 5-7.

339.

"SOVIET 'SPY LORIES' IN EUROPE"

The Economist. Foreign Report, 15 March 1978, pp. 3-4.

340.

"TSCHERNENKO - 'DIE RACHE DES APPARATS'"

[Chernenko - The Revenge of the Apparat]

Der Spiegel, 20 February 1984, pp. 118-28.

Identifies the then CPSU General Secretary Constantine Chernenko as the Deputy Chief of Personnel in the NKVD administration in Dnepropetrovsk in 1938/1939. According to this account, Chernenko participated in the execution of prisoners in the carwash garage of the local NKVD headquarters (p. 121). The author(s) of this piece may be referring, in part, to the 1958 Dneprovets' book Yezhovshchina (q.v.).

341.

"UNCONVENTIONAL WARFARE OPERATIONS"

Review of the Soviet Ground Forces, (Washington, D.C., Defense Intelligence Agency, October, 1981), pp. 3-6.

342.

**"YOUNG OFFICER WHO DEFECTED TO WEST IN 1974
DESCRIBES BRIEF CAREER AS KGB AGENT"**

Sunday Times (London), 16 January 1977, p. 9g.

An interview with Captain Aleksei Myagkov (q.v.).

343. AGURSKY, Mikhail and Hannes ADOMEIT

"THE SOVIET MILITARY-INDUSTRIAL COMPLEX"

Survey 24 (Spring 1979): pp. 106-124.

See pp. 110-114 for a succinct description of the
five-tiered Soviet system of classification and access
("dopusk"), controlled and administered throughout the
military-industrial and plant system by the KGB.

344. ANDERSON, Jack and Les WHITTEN

"KGB AGENTS CONCENTRATE ON THE HILL"

Washington Post, 30 June 1975, p. B9.

345. ANDREW, Christopher

**"THE BRITISH SECRET SERVICE AND ANGLO-SOVIET
RELATIONS IN THE 1920s. PART I: FROM THE TRADE
NEGOTIATIONS TO THE ZINOVIEV LETTER"**

The Historical Journal 20 (September 1977): pp.
673-706.

**"HOW BALDWIN'S SECRET SERVICE LOST THE SOVIET
CODE"**

Observer (London), 13 August 1978, pp. 17, 22.

Noteworthy analyses.

346. AVTORKHANOV, Abdurakhman

"V CHYOM SMYAL PEREIMENOVANNIYA KGB?"

[What is the Significance of the Change in the Name of the KGB?]

Posev (Munich), no. 9 (September 1978), pp. 3-5.

Incisive comment on the KGB's redesignation in July 1978.

347. AZRAEL, Jeremy

"AN END TO COERCION?"

Problems of Communism 11 (November-December 1962): pp. 9-11.

348. BARGHOORN, Frederick

"THE SECURITY POLICE"

In Interest Groups in Soviet Politics, H. Gordon Skilling and Franklyn Griffiths, eds.

Princeton, New Jersey: Princeton University Press for the Centre for Russian and East European Studies at the University of Toronto, 1971, pp. 93-129.

Recommended short overview. See also by the same author, "Justice...Police Formations", Chapter IX: pp. 346-61 in Politics in the USSR (Boston, Massachusetts, 1966), and "Rule Adjudication: Socialist Legality in Action", Chapter 10: pp. 275-307 in Politics in the USSR, 2nd Edition (1972).

349. BARRON, John

"ESPIONAGE: THE DARK SIDE OF DETENTE"

Reader's Digest 112 (January 1978): pp. 78-82.

Updates one of the themes of his first KGB book: expanding Soviet and Bloc intelligence and security service presence in the US.

"THE INHERITOR: A TALE OF KGB ESPIONAGE IN AMERICA" [LUDICK ZEMENEK AKA RUDOLF HERMANN AKA DOUGLAS]

Reader's Digest 120 (March 1982): pp. 191-242.

Describes the recruitment, training, vetting and emplacement of a long-term KGB illegal in Canada and the US.

350. BARROS, James

"ALGER HISS AND HARRY DEXTER WHITE: THE CANADIAN CONNECTION"

Orbis 21 (Fall 1977): pp. 593-605.

351. BARRY, DONALD D.; F.J.M. FELDBRUGGE; G. GINSBURGS; and P.B. MAGGS, eds.

"SOVIET LAW AFTER STALIN: SOVIET INSTITUTIONS AND THE ADMINISTRATION OF LAW"

Law in Eastern Europe 3 (1979): pp. 428.

352. BEN-SHLOMO, Zeev

"THE KHRUSHCHEV APOCRYPHA"

Soviet Jewish Affairs (London) 1 (June 1971): pp. 52-75.

353. BERG, Ger P. van den

"THE COUNCIL OF MINISTERS OF THE SOVIET UNION"

Review of Socialist Law 6 (September 1980): pp. 293-323.

A basic review and analysis of the background and legislative analysis of the 1978 law on the USSR Council of Ministers.

354. BINDER, David

"DETENTE IS SAID TO GIVE THE KGB A BIGGER WORK LOAD"

New York Times, 2 June 1975, p. 14.

355. BLACKSTOCK, Paul W.

"'BOOKS FOR IDIOTS': FALSE SOVIET 'MEMOIRS'"

The Russian Review 25 (July 1966): pp. 285-96.

356. BORCHGRAVE, Arnaud de

"UNSPIKING SOVIET TERRORISM"

International Security Review 8 (Spring 1982): pp. 3-16.

English translation and original text of an official French intelligence report on international terrorism, including Soviet links and support, obtained by the author from the Director General of the SDECE, Alexandre de Marenches on May 11, 1978. Jacques Duclos is stated (p. 10) to have been at one stage the secret head of the Curiel network, which is described in some detail. It should be recalled that Leon Trotsky openly declared that Duclos was "a GPU agent." See Jean van Heijenoort, With Trotsky in Exile (q.v.).

357. BURFORD, R.E.

"GETTING THE BUGS OUT OF SOCIALIST LEGALITY"

American Journal of Comparative Law 22 (Summer 1974): pp. 465-508.

358. CANADIAN BROADCASTING CORPORATION

"THE KGB CONNECTIONS: AN INVESTIGATION INTO SOVIET ESPIONAGE OPERATIONS IN NORTH AMERICA"

Transcript, 8 June 1981, pp. 59.

The most insightful and effective television presentation on KGB operations abroad.

359. CARON, Yves

"RADO: HISTOIRE D'UN GRANDE RESEAU SOVIETIQUE D'ESPIONAGE"

[Rado: History of a Great Soviet Espionage Network]

Est et Ouest [Paris], no. 662 (April 1982), pp. 446-452.

Well-informed factual review and biography on the occasion of Alexander Rado's death.

360. CARYNNIK, Marco

"THE FAMINE THE 'TIMES' COULDN'T FIND"

Commentary 76 (November 1983): pp. 32-40.

Regarding the New York Times correspondent in Moscow, Walter Duranty, and the famine in the Ukraine, 1933-1934.

361. CECIL, Robert

"LEGENDS SPIES TELL"

Encounter 50 (April 1978): pp. 9-17.

A pithy corrective to some of the more indulgent myths surrounding the Soviet agents Philby, Burgess and Maclean.

362. CLAUDIUS, W.

"IN A SOVIET ISOLATOR"

St. Antony's Papers - Soviet Affairs (London), no. 1 (1956), pp. 133-46.

"In the case of the MGB (CHEKA)...the brutality is collective and based almost on scientific research. Interrogators are trained in every step of brutality, but employ it only on special orders. Personally the MGB interrogator could be a nice chap..." (p. 133). An early eyewitness account.

363. COCKERELL, Michael

"WHO KILLED GEORGI MARKOV?"

Boston, Massachusetts: WGBH Transcripts, 1979, pp. 24.

The transcript of the PBS "World" television documentary on the "poisoned umbrella" assassination of Bulgarian defector Georgi Markov in London, September 1978. See also Markov's The Truth That Killed (q.v.).

364. CONQUEST, Robert

"A QUESTION OF SECURITY"

Soviet Analyst 6 (August 11, 1977): pp. 1-3.

Offers useful commentary on the inter-locking personal and family relations between Brezhnev and the top KGB leadership. It is the first public revelation that S.K. Tsvigun was Brezhnev's brother-in-law.

"THE HISTORIOGRAPHY OF THE PURGES"

Survey 22 (Winter 1976): pp. 157-164.

An important investigatory contribution to the record of the secret trials in Moscow from October 1937 to February 1939.

365. COOX, Alvin D.

"L'AFFAIRE LYUSHKOV: ANATOMY OF A DEFECTOR"

Soviet Studies 19 (January 1968): pp. 405-20.

A detailed presentation of the scantily available case history data on NKVD General G.S. Lyushkov who defected to Japanese forces in Manchuria in June 1938.

366. CROZIER, Brian

"AID FOR TERRORISM"

Annual of Power and Conflict 1973-1974

London, England: Institute for the Study of
Conflict, 1974, pp. 105.

For a description of Soviet Security and Intelligence
linkages to international terrorists, see pp. 2-11.

"THE PEACETIME STRATEGY OF THE SOVIET UNION"

Institute for the Study of Conflict Special
Report, February-March 1973, pp. 83.

See pp. 6-9: "Soviet Espionage Machinery: KGB and GRU";
"Growth of Intelligence Activities"; and three gra-
phics: "Soviet Presence in Europe in 1972 Showing
Strength of Intelligence Representatives" (by function, p. 41, by country pp. 42-43) and "Percentage
Increase of Soviet Representatives in Europe, 1961-1962
to 1972".

367. DAVIES, Derek

"THE KGB IN ASIA (PART I)"

Far Eastern Economic Review 93 (January 3, 1975):
pp. 20-3, 26-7.

"THE KGB IN ASIA (PART II)"

Far Eastern Economic Review 94 (December 31,
1976): pp. 20-34.

A retrospective follow-up to the survey done by the
same publication on January 3, 1975. The two articles
are a systematic expose of Soviet intelligence and
security services' operating bases in the Far East.

368. DEBO, Richard K.

"LOCKHART PLOT OR DZERZHINSKIY PLOT?"

Journal of Modern History 42 (September 1971): pp.
413-439.

369. DEDERICHS, Mario R. and Katherine HORBATSCH

"DIE 'SAUBERIN HANDE' DES GENOSSEN A."

[The 'Clean Hands' of Comrade A.]

Stern 35 (November 25, 1982): pp. 228-32.

"How Yuri Andropov transformed the KGB secret service
from a terror force to a subtle repressive system and
exploited it for his rise to Chief of the Party." A
very detailed and descriptive graphic of the KGB
accompanies the discussion.

370. DUBROW, Eldridge

"SOVIET AIMS: NEITHER WHOLLY A RIDDLE, NOR
MYSTERY, AND EVEN LESS AN ENIGMA"

Security and Intelligence Fund, Situation Report,
no. 4, Part I, pp. 8; Part II, pp. 7.

371. DUCOLI, John

"THE GEORGIAN PURGES, 1951-1953"

Caucasian Review (Munich), no. 6 (1958), pp.
54-61.

Discusses the Mingrelian case.

372. DUEVEL, Christian

"ADDITIONAL LIGHT ON THE BERIA CASE"

Radio Liberty Research CRD 28/72 (January 27,
1972): pp. 9.

See also entry #444, for a follow-up survey in 1983.

"THE NUMBER OF KGB AND MVD OFFICIALS IN BREZHNEV'S ENTOURAGE INCREASES"

Radio Liberty Research RL 156/77 (June 24, 1977): pp. 2.

373. DUNCAN, Susanna

"'STONE', THE MAN WHO WARNED ABOUT THE MOLES" (NOSENKO: THE RED HERRING, "FEDORA": THE SPY WHO DUPED J. EDGAR HOOVER, CHEREPANOV: THE WOULD-BE MOLE)

Interview by Edward J. Epstein

New York 11 (Februry 27, 1978): pp. 28-32, 34-8.

"OSWALD THE SECRET AGENT"

New York 11 (March 6, 1978): pp. 55-58.

374. DZIAK, John J.

"SOVIET INTELLIGENCE AND SECURITY SERVICES IN THE 1980s: THE PARA-MILITARY DIMENSION"

In Intelligence Requirements for the 1980's: Counterintelligence, Roy Godson, ed.

Washington, D.C.: National Strategy Information Center, Inc., 1980, pp. 95-115.

Analysis of the "Spetsnaz" (Special Purpose Forces) in the Soviet Security Service's direct action tradition was also published under the same title in ORBIS, Winter 1981, pp. 771-786.

THE ACTION ARM OF THE CPSU

Problems of Communism, July-August 1981, pp. 53-58.

A review of six relatively recent works dealing with Soviet intelligence and security. See also entries under Myagkov, Sakharov, Brook-Shepherd, Gerson, Rositzke and the Permanent Select Committee on Intelligence.

"THE SOVIET APPROACH TO SPECIAL OPERATIONS"

In Special Operations in U.S. Strategy. Frank R. Barnett, B. Hugh Tovar, and Richard H. Shultz, eds. Washington, D.C.: National Defense Univerity Press in Cooperation with the National Strategy Information Center, Inc., 1984, pp. 95-133.

A revisit of the "Spetsnaz" problem addressed in the Counterintelligence work above.

375. EINFRANK, Aaron R.

"FOREIGN CORRESPONDENTS IN THE USSR: THE UNWRITTEN CONDITIONS OF EMPLOYMENT"

Radio Liberty Research RL 32/77 (Feburary 8, 1977): pp. 5.

An expose of the rarely discussed KGB-ridden Directorate of the Soviet Foreign Office for the Servicing of the Diplomatic Corps (UPDK) in Moscow.

376. EPSTEIN, Edward Jay

"AN INCREDIBLE MOLE WHO WOULD BE TSAR" [Michael Goleniewski]

Washington Star, 17 May 1981, pp. G1, 4.

"THE RIDDLE OF ARMAND HAMMER"

New York Times Magazine, 23 November 1981, pp. 68-73, 112, 114, 116, 118, 120, 122.

"WHEN THE CIA WAS ALMOST WRECKED"

Parade Magazine (Washington Post), 14 October 1984, pp. 8-11s.

A review of the Golitsyn case and the resultant associated investigations of the CIA, FBI, and British and French services. See Golitsyn's New Lies for Old (q.v.) for his views of the Soviet strategy behind the alleged penetrations.

377. FAIRBANKS, Charles H. Jr.

"NATIONAL CADRES AS A FORCE IN THE SOVIET SYSTEM: THE EVIDENCE OF BERIA'S CAREER, 1949-53"

In Soviet Nationality Policies and Practices, Jeremy R. Azrael, ed. (New York, New York: 1958), pp. 144-85.

"BERIA, HIS ENEMIES AND THEIR GEORGIAN CLIENTELES, 1949-1953"

The Wilson Center. Kennan Institute for Advanced Russian Studies, Smithsonian Institution Bldg., Washington, D.C., 1980. Occasional Paper, no. 119, pp. 49.

378. FEDORCHUK, Vitaliy Vasil'evich

"UKRAINIAN KGB CHIEF WARNS OF IDEOLOGICAL SABOTAGE"

Radio Liberty Research RL 422/81 (October 22, 1981): pp. 4.

A detailed commentary on two vigilance-theme articles authored by Fedorchuk (now the MVD Chief) in October 1981. Both appeared in Ukrainian journals shortly before he began his brief tenure as KGB chairman.

379. FRANTZELL, Lennart

"THE NTS. THE ENEMY WITHIN"

National Review 10 (July 1981): p. 783.

A favorable presentation on the activity of the Narodno Trudovoy Soyuz (NTS), a Russian emigre association formed in the early 1930s "to offer a democratic alternative to the Soviet Communist Party".

380. FULLER, Elizabeth

   **"TRANSCAUCASIAN KGB CHIEFS WARN AGAINST IDEO-
   LOGICAL SUBVERSION"**

   Radio Liberty Research RL 5/81 (January 5, 1981):
   pp. 3.

Summarizes and comments upon two articles by KGB chiefs
of Azerbaijan and Armenia, Major General Ziya Yusif-
Zade and Major General Marius Yuzbashyan.

381. GAYEV, Arkady G.

   "THE NOBLE CHEKISTS"

   Bulletin of the Munich Institute for the Study of
   the USSR 12 (March 1965): pp. 18-21.

An early discussion of KGB enhanced image projection.

382. GIDWITZ, Betsy

   **"ASPECTS OF SOVIET INTERNATIONAL CIVIL AVIATION
   POLICY"**

   Survey 24 (Spring 1979): pp. 19-44.

On Aeroflot participation in the 1968 occupation of
Czechoslovakia, and involvement in the performance of
espionage.

383. GILLETTE, Robert

   "'SUICIDE' HINTS OF NEW SOVIET POWER STRUGGLE"

   Los Angeles Times, 2 March 1982, p. 1.

Reports rumors that the death in early 1982 of General
Tsvigun (First Deputy Chief, KGB) was by suicide and
was associated with the opening rounds of the succession struggle for Brezhnev's position.

384. GLENNY, Michael and Bolidan R. BOCIURKIW

"POLITICAL DISSENT IN THE SOVIET UNION"

Studies in Comparative Communism 3 (April 1970):
pp. 65-148.

385. HARISYMIW, B.

"NOMENCLATURA: THE SOVIET COMMUNIST PARTY'S
RECRUITMENT SYSTEM"

Canadian Journal of Political Science 2 (December
1969): pp. 493-512.

386. HARRISS, Joseph A.

"THE KREMLIN VS. THE CHURCH"

Reader's Digest 119 (September 1981): pp. 113-17.

387. HEIMAN, Leo

"CLOAK AND DAGGER LITERATURE BEHIND THE IRON
CURTAIN"

East Europe 14 (January 14, 1965): pp. 54-56.

"THE PRIEST WITH THE FALSE BEARD"

American Legion Magazine 70 (April 1961): pp.
20-1, 46-7.

A detailed account of Soviet utilization of Greek
Orthodox church delegations in Israel.

388. HELLER, Michael

"STALIN AND THE DETECTIVES"

Survey 211 (Winter-Spring 1975): pp. 160-175.

An acute examination and survey of the political thrust of the literary output in the USSR on security and intelligence themes.

389. HERNDON, James S. and Joseph O. BAYLEN

> "COL. PHILIP R. FAYMONVILLE AND THE RED ARMY, 1934-1943"
>
> Slavic Review 34 (September 1975): pp. 483-505.

Faymonville was the first US military attache to the USSR. His involvement with the Soviet military from 1934 to 1943 was accompanied by controversy and the "taint of being overly sympathetic to the Soviets" (p. 504). See also entry #400.

390. HINKLE, Warren

> "THE MYSTERY OF THE BLACK BOOKS"
>
> Esquire 79 (April 1973): pp. 128-31, 170, 172, 174.

See also Hinkle's An Essential Memoir of a Lunatic Decade (q.v.).

391. HOOK, Sidney

> "THE INCREDIBLE STORY OF MICHAEL STRAIGHT"
>
> Encounter 61 (December 1983): pp. 68-73.

392. JAFFE, Phillip J.

> "AGNES SMEDLEY: A REMINISCENCE"
>
> Survey 20 (Autumn 1974): pp. 172-79.

393. JAMESON, Donald

"TRENDS IN SOVIET COVERT ACTION"

In Intelligence Requirements of the 1980s: Covert Action, Roy Godson, ed.

Washington, D.C.: National Strategy Information Center, 1981, pp. 169-190.

See also follow up article by same writer: "The Clandestine Battlefield: Trenches and Trends", Strategic Review 11 (Winter 1983): pp. 19-28.

394. JORDAN, Henry

"IVAN SEROV: HATCHET MAN FOR THE KREMLIN"

Reader's Digest 72 (February 1958): pp. 121-22, 124, 126, 129.

A condensation and revision by the author of an article which appeared originally in Argosy (December 1959). Citing the State Security defector, Lt. Col. Burlutsky: "He [Serov] is the most ruthless, most opportunistic swine in the whole dirty business".

395. KLEPIKOVA, Elena and Vladimir SOLOVYOV

"THE SECRET RUSSIAN PARTY"

translated by Guy Daniels

Midstream 26 (October 1980): pp. 12-19.

Allegations of Great Russian nationalism permeating Party, military and government including Intelligence and Security Services, asserted by two emigre writers.

396. KNIGHT, Amy W.

"SOVIET POLITICS AND THE KGB/MVD RELATIONSHIP"

Soviet Union/Union Sovietique 11 [Part II] (1984): pp. 157-81.

"THE KGB'S SPECIAL DEPARTMENTS IN THE SOVIET ARMED
FORCES"

Orbis 28 (Summer 1984): pp. 257-80.

"ANDROPOV: MYTHS AND REALITIES"

Survey 28 (Spring 1984): pp. 22-44.

"PYOTR MASHEROV AND THE SOVIET LEADERSHIP: A STUDY
IN KREMLINOLOGY"

Survey 26 (Winter 1982): pp. 151-68.

"THE POWERS OF THE SOVIET KGB"

Survey 25 (Summer 1980): pp. 138-55.

These articles are important contributions to an
understanding of the KGB's status and role under
Brezhnev and Andropov.

397. KRAMER, Arnold

"RUSSIAN COUNTERFEIT DOLLARS: A CASE OF EARLY
SOVIET ESPIONAGE"

Slavic Review 30 (December 1971): pp. 762-73.

Recounts Stalin's effort to counterfeit US $100 notes
in 1928 utilizing both the Comintern and Soviet
military intelligence. Although the scheme was a fiasco
it did not end until 1934. A basic survey piece. See
also, Krivitsky (q.v.).

398. KRASIN, Victor

"HOW I WAS BROKEN BY THE KGB"

New York Times Magazine, 18 March 1984, pp. 53-4,
68, 70-1, 73, 76, 77.

399. KUSTOVTSEV, R.

"NELEGAL'NIYE UKHODI IZ SSSR"

[Illegal Departures from the USSR]

Posev (Munich), no. 7 (1978), pp. 24-28.

Statistics and commentary on post-World War II Soviet defection (to 1969). Based on a sample of 600 cases.

400. LANGER, John David

"THE 'RED GENERAL': PHILLIP R. FAYMONVILLE... 1917-1952"

Prologue 8 (Winter 1976): pp. 208-24.

See also entry # 389.

401. LAPENNA, Ivo

"THE CONTEMPORARY CRISES ON LEGALITY IN THE SOVIET UNION: SUBSTANTIVE CRIMINAL LAW"

Review of Socialist Law (The Hague) 1 (1975): pp. 71, 73-95.

402. LEGGETT, George

"LENIN, TERROR AND THE POLITICAL POLICE"

Survey 97 (Autumn 1975): pp. 157-87.

"THE CHEKA AND A CRISIS OF COMMUNIST CONSCIENCE"

Survey 25 (Summer 1980): pp. 122-37.

Two basic surveys of an important aspect of the ethos and the method of the Soviet security service.

142

403. LERCH, I.A.

"EFFECTIVE INTERNATIONAL CO-OPERATION"

Science 212 (June 5, 1981): p. 1085.

Deals with the accusation of espionage by the Soviet, A. Belozerov, while he was in Vienna. His case highlights KGB utilization of international scientific co-operative organizations as operational cover.

404. LOEBER, Dietrich A.

"STATUTES OF AGENCIES WITH MINISTERIAL STATUS IN THE USSR: LIST OF SOURCES AS OF 1 JULY 1982"

Review of Socialist Law 8 (December 1982): pp. 359-67.

For a discussion of the KGB's unpublished statute, see p. 363 and footnote 46.

"THE SOVIET PROCURACY AND THE RIGHTS OF THE INDIVIDUAL AGAINST THE STATE"

Journal of the International Commission of Jurists 1 (Autumn 1957): pp. 59-105.

405. MAITLAND, Leslie

"NEW YORK TERMED 'HUB' OF FOREIGN SPIES IN U.S."

New York Times, 14 November 1981.

Includes details on order of battle and modus operandi of Soviet intelligence and security in New York. See also, Harry Rositzke. "Why the KGB Loves New York...", Washington Post, 28 March 1982, pp. C1, C4.

406. MASTERMAN, S.

"CHARGED WITH SPYING, RUSSIAN PHYSICIST QUITS INTERNATIONAL INSTITUTE"

Chronicle of Higher Education 22 (May 1981): pp. 13-14.

Another article on the case of A. Belozerov. See also
article by I.A. Lerch (q.v.).

407. MAUNY, Erik de

   **"VICTOR LOUIS, LE TRAPEZISTE DE LA DESINFOR-
   MATION"**

   [Victor Louis, the Trapeze Artist of Disinfor-
   mation]

   L'Express, 5 May 1981, pp. 90-93.

An informed review of Louis' activity by the former BBC
correspondent in Moscow.

408. McNEILL, Terry

   "THE KREMLIN, KIROV AND THE COVER-UP"

   Radio Liberty Research RL 216/76 (April 26, 1976):
   pp. 11.

On the 1934 assassination of Sergei Kirov and the
continued Party cover-up.

409. MEDVEDEV, Roy

   **"REQUIEM FOR A TRAITOR: A SPY'S LONELY LOYALTY TO
   OLD, BETRAYED IDEALS"**

   Washington Post, 19 June 1983, pp. B1, 4.

On the death of Donald MacLean in Moscow: "...those
who knew him best, respected him and considered him a
sincere person whose fate was not only unusual, but
tragic...he was one of the best spies who ever worked
for Soviet intelligence."

410. MIHALKA, Michael

"SOVIET STRATEGIC DECEPTION, 1955-1981"

Journal of Strategic Studies (London) 1 (1981):
pp. 40-93.

Also reprinted in Military Deception and Strategic
Surprises, John Goach and Amos Perlmutter, eds.
(London, French Cass and Company Ltd., 1982, pp.
40-93).

411. MOSS, Robert

"THE CAMPAIGN TO DESTABILIZE IRAN"

Conflict Studies, no. 101 (November 1978), pp.
17.

See pp. 4-7: "Soviet Espionage Operations". An extended
discussion of the cases of General Ahmed Mogharabi and
Ali Naghi Rabbani, Soviet agents.

"HOW RUSSIA PLOTS AGAINST THE SHAH"

Sunday Telegraph (London), 5 November 1978.

Besides the cases noted above, this article takes up
the arrest, in April 1978, of the retired General Ali
Akbar Darakhani.

"INSIDE THE GRU"

Parade Magazine (Washington Post), 6 September
1981, pp. 7-9.

A neglected topic is surveyed with some small flaws in
historical detail.

"SPIES OF SOVIET GENERAL STAFF"

Daily Telegraph (London), 1 June 1981.

Another, complementary treatment of the GRU.

"WHAT RUSSIA WANTS. DEFINING SOVIET DESIGNS IN CENTRAL ASIA"

The New Republic, 19 January 1980, pp. 23-25.

412. MOTYL, Alexander J.

"ROY MEDVEDEV: DISSIDENT OR CONFORMIST?"

Survey 25 (Summer 1980): pp. 74-85.

413. MOWBRAY, Stephen de

SOVIET DECEPTION AND THE ONSET OF THE COLD WAR: THE BRITISH DOCUMENTS FOR 1943--A LESSON IN MANIPULATION

Encounter 62 July-August 1984, pp. 16-24.

Discusses Soviet strategic political deception in the period 1943-1945 and the concomitant roles of Communists, near Communists and Soviet agents in influencing official British thinking and therefore policy towards the USSR. The author argues that the tradition continues in an updated and more sophisticated fashion transcending the low-level techniques of tactical disinformation such as forgeries.

414. MURPHY, Carlyle and Alison MUSCATINE

"POLITE WAR: SOVIET SPIES IN OUR MIDST"

Washington Post, 19 June 1983, pp. 1A, 12.

Expose of the KGB Washington Residentura and the Rezident, Stanoslav A. Androsov.

415. NEKRICH, Alexander

"THE SOVIET-GERMAN TREATY OF AUGUST 1939"

(Cambridge, Massachusetts, Russian Research Center) 18 May 1977, FAR paper (Office of External Research, US Department of State), pp. 15.

416. NEL, Phillip R.

"SOVIET AFRICAN DIPLOMACY AND THE ROLE OF THE INTERNATIONAL DEPARTMENT"

African Insight 12 (1982): pp. 132-141.

Argues forcefully for an overarching and supervisory role for the CPSU's International Department in Soviet African policy in which the KGB and the military play the role of executors. Nel builds on the late Leonard Schapiro's earlier piece on the International Department in International Journal (Winter, 1976-1977). See entry #431.

417. OLCUTT, Martha B.

"THE BASMACHI OR FREEMAN'S REVOLT IN TURKESTAN 1918-1924"

Soviet Studies 33 (July 1981): pp. 352-69.

Notes the utilization of specified security service (OGPU) troops in the suppression of the Turkestan revolt, 1931.

418. PANOFF, Kyrill

"MURDER ON WATERLOO BRIDGE: THE CASE OF GEORGI MARKOV"

Encounter 53 (November 1979): pp. 15-21.

419. PARHAM, William F.

"CASTRO'S AGENTS SPY FOR THE SOVIETS"

Norwich (Sunday) Bulletin (Connecticut), 23, 24, 25, 26, 27 August 1981.

This five-part series contains a detailed review based on seat-of-government interviews.

"SOVIET DECEPTION"

<u>Norwich Bulletin</u> (Connecticut), 21, 22, 24 February 1982.

This three part series is an intriguing account of the use of "active measures" by the Soviet and Polish Security Services in the crushing of Solidarity in December 1981. It includes details of Soviet intelligence <u>modus operandi</u>.

"KGB SPARES NO EXPENSE ON EVESDROPPING IN U.S."

"THERE ISN'T MUCH THE KGB EVESDROPPERS CAN'T HEAR"

"HOW MUCH CAN THE KGB HEAR?"

<u>Norwich Bulletin</u> (Connecticut), 18, 19, 20 April 1982.

420. PARROT, Bruce

"TECHNOLOGICAL PROGRESS AND SOVIET POLITICS"

<u>Survey</u> 2 (Spring 1977-1978), pp. 39-60.

The author develops the controversial thesis that the KGB sees contacts between Soviet citizens and foreigners as a considerable political danger not outweighed by the concomitant economic and technological benefits.

421. PONYATOVSKY, K.

"MODERN SCIENCE IN THE SERVICE OF THE NKVD"

<u>Ukrainian Quarterly</u> 8 (Autumn 1952): pp. 347-51.

422. REED, D.

"EAST GERMANY'S SINISTER SUPERSPOOK"

<u>Reader's Digest</u> 117 (December 1980): pp. 173-76.

The subject of this article is Markus Wolf, Chief of the Hauptverwaltung Aufklarung, the intelligence component of the East German security ministry.

423. REES, John

   "INFILTRATION OF THE MEDIA BY THE KGB AND ITS FRIENDS"

   In Accuracy in Media Conference, Washington, D.C., 20 April 1978, pp. 37.

A documented synthesis of the record of sworn testimony and uncontroverted memoir dealing with past Soviet security activity in the US.

424. REES, Mervyn

   "THE SPY WHO KNEW IT ALL"

   Daily Mail (London), 20 November 1983, pp. 1-2, 31-4.

An in-depth account of the recent case of Commodore Dieter Gerhardt, a long-standing Soviet penetration of the South African naval establishment.

425. REITZ, James T.

   "THE SOVIET SECURITY TROOPS- THE KREMLIN'S OTHER ARMIES"

   In Soviet Armed Forces Review Annual 6 (1982): pp. 279-327.

   Gulf Breeze, Florida: Academic International Press, 1982, pp. 431.

See pp. 279-327 for rare and sound coverage of a little known aspect of Soviet military-security power: the troops not under the Ministry of Defense, but at the disposal of the Party for its exclusive purposes--the troops of the KGB and the MVD.

426. ROSEFELDT, Steven

"AN ASSESSMENT OF THE SOURCES AND USES OF GULAG
FORCED LABOR, 1929-1956"

Soviet Studies 33 (January 1981): pp. 51-87.

A carefully researched piece on the size, scope and
time profile of Soviet forced labor for the period
1929-1956. "From 1934-1956, GULAG workers on average
constituted more than 20% of the nonagricultural labor
force, diminishing thereafter". It confirms findings of
Conquest, D. Dallin, Swianiewicz and Solzhenitsyn.
Compare with Wheatcroft (q.v.).

427. ROWAN, Roy

"THE DEATH OF DAVE KARR AND OTHER MYSTERIES"

Fortune 100 (December 3, 1979): pp. 94-6, 99-102,
104, 106, 108

428. SAFIRE, William

"MY NOMEN IS KLATURA"

The New York Times Magazine, 14 October 1984, pp.
14-16.

A tongue-in-cheek etymological evisceration of Moscow's
system for the maintenance of class privilege.

429. SAKHAROV, Vladimir

"SPECIAL ISSUE ON THE SOVIET ROLE IN INTERNATIONAL
TERRORISM, PROPAGANDA AND INFLUENCE ACTIVITIES"

HUMINT (The Human Intelligence Network Report) 1
(May 15, 1981): pp. 12.

See also entry #133.

430. SATTER, David

"THE NEW GULAG: SOVIET DISSIDENTS DIE OF MEDICAL NEGLECT"

Wall Street Journal, 30 October 1984, p. 30.

Presents evidence that Soviet political prisoners are now (1983/84) being allowed to die through the withholding of medicines and medical treatment.

431. SCHAPIRO, Leonard

"THE GENERAL DEPARTMENT OF THE CENTRAL COMMITTEE OF THE CPSU"

Survey 21 (Summer 1975): pp. 53-65.

An important article. Traces the founding and the development under Stalin of a significant piece of party machinery for the coordination of Security Service organization, personnel and operations, at times known as the "Secret Department" and the "Special Sektor". The General Department was headed from 1928 to 1953 by A.N. Poskrebyshev.

"THE INTERNATIONAL DEPARTMENT OF THE CPSU: KEY TO SOVIET POLICY"

International Journal 33 (Winter 1976-1977): pp. 41-58.

A trenchant presentation by the authoritative, recently deceased, British analyst of Soviet Party history and organization: "...Soviet foreign policy, far from being torn by Party-State rivalry, is a unified, coordinated whole in which, after Brezhnev, the leading central role belongs to the International Department of the Central Committee of the CPSU..."

432. SCORER, Alexandre

"THE KGB"

Listener (London) 91 (February 14, 1974): pp. 204-207.

151

A most effective 90 minute television documentary by the BBC in mid-February 1974.

433. SERVICE, R.J.

"THE ROAD TO THE TWENTIETH PARTY CONGRESS: AN ANALYSIS OF THE EVENTS SURROUNDING THE CENTRAL COMMITTEE PLENUM OF JULY 1953" [THE FORGOTTEN PLENUM, 2-7 July 1953]

Soviet Studies 33 (April 1981): pp. 232-45.

434. SEVIN, Dieter

"OPERATION SCHERHORN"

Military Review 46 (March 1966): pp. 35-43.

A summary account of a radio playback/deception operation conducted by the Soviets on the Eastern Front. Purportedly, Colonel Scherhorn and 2,500 men had been isolated and surrounded at Beresino. The operation was played successfully by the Soviets to induce the commitment of German supplies and forces in futile and costly recovery efforts.

435. SLUSSER, Robert M.

"CHEKIST LEADERS FROM DZERZHINSKIY TO YEZHOV: VARIATIONS ON A THEME"

San Francisco, California: American Historical Association, 29 December 1973, pp. 12.

Paper delivered at a meeting of the American Historical Association in San Francisco, December 29, 1973.

"RECENT SOVIET BOOKS ON THE HISTORY OF THE SOVIET SECURITY POLICE"

Slavic Review 14 (March 1965): pp. 90-98.

"RECENT SOVIET BOOKS ON THE HISTORY OF THE SOVIET
SECURITY POLICE-- PART II"

Slavic Review 22 (December 1973): pp. 825-28.

436. SOLOVYOV, Vladimir

"KNOWING THE KGB"

Partisan Review 49 (1982), pp. 167-83.

A most insightful, monitory appraisal.

437. SOUTHERLAND, Daniel

"SPY WARS: THE GLOBAL STRUGGLE FOR POWER"

Christian Science Monitor, 22-26, 29 September
1980.

A six-part survey of the status, organization and
operations, mainly based on anecdote and secondary
materials, of world espionage. The KGB is examined in
Part II, "The Soviet Union's Principal Intelligence
Agency", 23 September 1980, p. 11.

438. STEINER, George

"REFLECTIONS: THE CLERIC OF TREASON"

The New Yorker, 8 December 1980, pp. 160-95.

A mordant portrait of Anthony Blunt, Soviet agent.

439. SUVOROV, Victor

"SPETSNAZ: THE SOVIET UNION'S SPECIAL FORCES"

International Defense Review (Geneva) 16 (September 1983): pp. 8.

Details on GRU (Soviet Military Intelligence) responsibility for Spetsnaz organization, training and
peace-time planning.

153

440. SZULC, Tad

"WHY THE RUSSIANS ARE TRYING HARDER TO STEAL OUR SECRETS"

Parade Magazine (Washington Post), 7 November 1982, pp. 14-15, 17.

441. TARABOCHIA, Alfonso L.

"A RED AXIS IN THE CARIBBEAN? THE SOVIET-CUBAN EXPANSIONISM IN AMERICA'S BACKYARD"

Gaithersburg, Maryland: International Chiefs of Police,Inc., Bureau of Operations and Research, Group and Area Studies, Vol. 8, 1983, pp. 22.

An authoritative account by a former staff member of the Senate Internal Security Subcommittee.

442. TERRY, Anton and Philip KNIGHTLY

"THE HOUSEWIFE WHO SPIED FOR RUSSIA"

Sunday Times (London), 29 June 1980.

The story of Ruth Kucynski, aka Sonya, aka Ruth Werner. See also entry #150. A GRU illegal, radio equipped, "Sonya" was in the UK as Klaus Fuchs' contact from the end of 1941 until his departure for the US in November 1943. See Chapman Pincher, Too Secret Too Long (q.v.).

443. TILLET, Lowell

"UKRAINIAN NATIONALISM AND THE FALL OF SHELEST"

Slavic Review 34 (December 1975): pp. 752-68.

444. TOLZ, Vladimir

"THE DEATH AND 'SECOND LIFE' OF LAVRENTIY BERIA"

Radio Liberty Research RL 47 9/83 (December 23, 1983): pp. 11.

"...examines the differing accounts of the arrest and execution of the most prominent figure in the Soviet State during the Stalinist period."

445. TRENTO, Joe and Dave ROMAN

"THE KGB IN NEW YORK"

Penthouse 9 (August 1978): pp. 63-4, 66.

446. VINOCUR, John

"THE KGB GOES ON THE OFFENSIVE, THE WEST BEGINS STRIKING BACK"

New York Times, 24 July 1983, pp. 2.

"A TRAIL OF WESTERN TECHNOLOGY IS FOLLOWED TO THE KGB'S DOOR"

New York Times, 25 July 1983, pp. 2.

"KGB OFFICERS TRY TO INFILTRATE ANTIWAR GROUPS"

New York Times, 26 July 1983, pp. 2.

447. VOLKMAN, Ernest

"THE SEARCH FOR SASHA: HAS A RUSSIAN MOLE INFILTRATED THE CIA"?

Family Weekly (Leavenworth Times), 9 October 1983.

448. WALKIN, Jacob

"SOME CONTRASTS BETWEEN THE TSARIST AND COMMUNIST POLITICAL SYSTEMS"

New Review of East European History (Toronto, Canada) 15 (March 1976): pp. 55-66.

This comparison of Tsarist and Soviet institutions and methods is an especially useful review of internal security practices of the two systems. Late Tsarist Russia pales beside its successor.

449. WEINSTEIN, Allen

"NADYA--A SPY STORY...CONVERSATION IN JERUSALEM"

Encounter 48 (June 1977): pp. 72-79.

A debriefing of the surviving member of the Soviet
(GRU) illegal team of Alexandre and Nadezhda Ulanovskiy. Alexandre Ulanovskiy is identical with Sorge's
original principal in Shanghai ("Alex") in 1930. For
the book by Allen Weinstein which includes this subject
and Nedezhda Ulanovskiy's own memoir, see Perjury: The
Hiss-Chambers Case (q.v.).

450. WELLES, Benjamin

"KGB: 9000 SOVIET SPIES HAVEN'T COME IN FROM THE
COLD"

Christian Science Monitor, 1 December 1975, pp.
22-3.

451. WHEATCROFT, S.G.

"ON ASSESSING THE SIZE OF FORCED CONCENTRATION
CAMP LABOUR IN THE SOVIET UNION"

Soviet Studies 33 (April 1981): pp. 265-95.

452. WISHNEVSKY, Julia

"INFORMATION ON THE OPERATIONS OF GLAVLIT SECTION
NO. 2"

Radio Liberty Research RL 494/76 (December 8,
1976): pp. 10.

Historical and current detail on the organization and
work of the Main Administration for the Safeguarding of
State and Defense Secrets in the Press.

453. YOUNG, Gregory D.

MUTINY ON STOROZHEVOY: A CASE STUDY OF DISSENT IN THE SOVIET NAVY

Monterey, California: Naval Postgraduate School, March 1982, pp. 125.

A close look, despite a lack of available detail, at the celebrated abortive mutiny on a Soviet destroyer.

454. ZASLAVSKY, Victor and Yuri LURYI

"THE PASSPORT SYSTEM IN THE USSR AND CHANGES IN SOVIET SOCIETY"

Soviet Union/Union Sovietique 6 (1979): pp. 137-53.

A detailed, informed statement about the control system and the implications of the recall and reissuance of Internal Passports to the whole population during the period 1976-1981.

455. ZEMSTZOV, Ilya

"KGB"

Two part article in Russian

Novoya Russkaya Slovo (New York), 16, 22 April 1978, pp. 7.

First-hand observations and commentary by a Soviet sociologist emigre, now in Israel.

Section Five

Congressional and Other Government Documents

456.   **U.S. CONGRESS, HOUSE,** Committee on Armed Services, CIA Subcommittee, Statement of Laszlo Szabo, 89th Congress, 2nd Session, 1966, (Washington DC, GPO), pp. 5331-5337.

457.   **U.S. CONGRESS, HOUSE,** Committee on Foreign Relations, Subcommittee on International Organizations, Psychiatric Abuse of Political Prisoners in the Soviet Union. Testimony of Leonid Plyushch, 94th Congress, 2nd Session, 1976, (Washington DC, GPO), pp. 1-81.

458.   **U.S. CONGRESS, HOUSE,** Permanent Select Committee on Intelligence, Subcommittee on Oversight, The CIA and the Media, CIA Report on Soviet Propaganda Operations, 95th Congress, 1st and 2nd Session, 1978, (Washington DC, GPO), pp. 531-627.

459.   **U.S. CONGRESS, HOUSE,** Permanent Select Committee on Intelligence, Subcommittee on Oversight, Soviet Covert Action (The Forgery Offensive), 96th Congress, 2nd Session, 1980, (Washington DC, GPO), pp. 245.

Most of the Hearings consist of testimony prepared by the CIA's Deputy Director for Operations, designed to provide an overview of recent Soviet political and propaganda covert action, with particular attention focused on the Soviet use of forgeries. It resumes, after a lengthy time gap, a line of testimony initiated by the then-Assistant CIA Director, Richard Helms, Senate Internal Security Subcommittee (1961) (see entry #495).

460.   **U.S. CONGRESS, HOUSE,** Permanent Select Com-
mittee on Intelligence, Subcommittee on
Oversight, Soviet Active Measures, 97th
Congress, 2nd Session, 1982, (Washington DC,
GPO), pp. 337.

461.   **U.S. CONGRESS, HOUSE,** Special Committee on
Un-American Activities, Investigation of
Un-American Propaganda Activities in the United
States. Testimony of Walter G. Krivitsky, 76th
Congress, 1st Session, 1939, (Washington DC,
GPO), pp. 5719-742.

462.   **U.S. CONGRESS, HOUSE,** Committee on Un-American
Activities. Testimony of Victor Kravchenko,
80th Congress, 1st Session, 1947, (Washington
DC, GPO), pp. 1-30.

463.   **U.S. CONGRESS, HOUSE,** Committee on Un-Amer-
ican Activities. Testimony of Gen. Izyador
Modelski, 81st Congress, 1st Session, 1949,
(Washington DC, GPO), pp. 1-100.

See also translations of instructions and other
documents submitted by Gen. Izydor Modelski, former
military attache of the Polish Embassy, Washington,
D.C., in U.S. CONGRESS, SENATE, Committee on the Judiciary, Subcommittee on Immigration and Naturalization,
Communist Activities Among Aliens and National Groups,
Part 3, Appendix III, 81st Congress, 1st Session, 1950,
pp. A11-A41. See also, entry #473.

464.   **U.S. CONGRESS, HOUSE,** Committee on Un-American
Activities, The Shameful Years: Thirty years of
Soviet Espionage in the United States, 82nd
Congress, 2nd Session, 1951-1952,(Washington
DC, GPO), pp. 70.

465.   **U.S. CONGRESS, HOUSE,** Committee on Un-American
Activities, Investigation of Communist Activities in the Los Angeles, California Area,
Part 8. Testimony of Nikolai Khokhlov: Dis-
content of Russian People With Communist
Leadership, 84th Congress, 1st and 2nd Sessions, 1956, (Washington DC, GPO), pp. 3755-
3820.

466.   **U.S. CONGRESS, HOUSE,** Committee on Un-American
        Activities, The Kremlin's Espionage and Terror
        Organizations. Testimony of Peter S. Deriabin,
        86th Congress, 1st Session, 1959, (Washington
        DC, GPO), pp. 1-16.

467.   **U.S. CONGRESS, HOUSE,** Committee on Un-Am-
        erican Activities. Testimony of Captain
        Nikolai Fedorovich Artamonov, 86th Congress,
        2nd Session, 1960, (Washington DC, GPO), pp.
        1903-1920.

468.   **U.S. CONGRESS, HOUSE,** Committee on Un-American
        Activities. Testimony of Wladyslaw Tykocinski,
        89th Congress, 2nd Session, 1966, (Washington
        DC, GPO), pp. 851-909.

469.   **U.S. CONGRESS, SENATE,** Commerce Committee,
        Soviet Oceans Development, paper of Carl
        Jacobsen, "The 'Civilian' Fleets: notes on
        Military-Civilian Integration in the USSR",
        Washington, D.C., GPO, October 1976, pp.
        257-285.

See p. 261 for characterization of the Party and KGB
abroad as comparable "to the role of chaplains aboard
Western vessels, in number and also in functions".

470.   **U.S. CONGRESS, SENATE,** Select Committee to
        Study Governmental Operations with Respect to
        Intelligence Activities, Final Report, Book 1,
        Foreign and Military Intelligence, 94th
        Congress, 2nd Session, 1976, (Washington DC,
        GPO), pp. 1-651.

This document will often be found listed as a general
Senate publication as this temporary committee was
quite short-lived. See pp. 557-61, "Soviet Intelligence Collection and Operations against the United
States."

471.   **U.S. CONGRESS, SENATE,** Select Committee on
        Intelligence, The Soviet Succession. Testimony
        of Prof. Jerry Hough, Prof. Myron Rush, Dr.
        Robert Conquest and Mr. William Hyland, 97th
        Congress, 2nd Session, 1982, (Washington DC,
        GPO), pp. 1-83

This document includes the declassified version (pp.
27-43) of CIA testimony at a closed Committee hearing,
28 September 1982.

472.   **U.S. CONGRESS, SENATE,** Committee on the
Judiciary, Subcommittee on Immigration and
Naturalization, Communist Activities Among
Alien And National Groups, Part I. Testimony of
Kirill Mikhailovich Alexeev, former Commercial
Air Attache, Soviet Embassy, Mexico, 81st
Congress, 1st Session, 1949, (Washington DC,
GPO), pp. 65-76.

473.   **U.S. CONGRESS, SENATE,** Committee on the
Judiciary, Subcommittee on Immigration and
Naturalization. Testimony of Gen. Izyador
Modelski, former military attache of Poland,
81st Congress, 2nd Session, 1950, (Washington
DC, GPO), pp. 6-29.

474.   **U.S. CONGRESS, SENATE,** Committee on the
Judiciary, Subcommittee to Investigate the
Administration of the Internal Security Act and
Other Internal Security Laws, Institute of
Pacific Relations, Part 1.   Testimony of
Alexandre Gregory Barmine, 82nd Congress, 1st
Session, 1951, (Washington DC, GPO), pp.
181-222.

475.   **U.S. CONGRESS, SENATE,** Committee on the
Judiciary, Subcommittee to Investigate the
Administration of the Internal Security Act and
Other Internal Security Laws, Institute of
Pacific Relations, Part 2. Testimony of
Whittaker Chambers, 82nd Congress, 1st and 2nd
Sessions, 1951-1952, (Washington DC, GPO), pp.
487-511, 4775-4804.

476.   **U.S. CONGRESS, SENATE,** Committee on the
Judiciary, Subcommittee to Investigate the
Administration of the Internal Security Act and
Other Internal Security Laws, Activities of
U.S. Citizens Employed by the United Nations.
Testimony of Whittaker Chambers, 82nd Congress,
2nd Session, 1952, (Washington DC, GPO), pp.
127-140.

477.   **U.S. CONGRESS, SENATE,** Committee on the
         Judiciary, Subcommittee to Investigate the
         Administration of the Internal Security Act and
         Other Internal Security Laws, <u>Institute of</u>
         <u>Pacific Relations, Part 2. Testimony of</u>
         <u>Elizabeth Bentley</u>, 82nd Congress, 1st and 2nd
         Sessions, 1951-1952, (Washington DC, GPO), pp.
         403-447, 487-511, 4775-4804.

478.   **U.S. CONGRESS, SENATE,** Committee on the
         Judiciary, Subcommittee to Investigate the
         Administration of the Internal Security Act and
         Other Internal Security Laws, <u>Institute of</u>
         <u>Pacific Relations, Part 1. Testimony of Mrs.</u>
         <u>Hede Massing</u>, 82nd Congress, 1st and 2nd
         Sessions, 1951-1952, (Washington DC, GPO), pp.
         223-341, 4798-4804.

479.   **U.S. CONGRESS, SENATE,** Committee on the
         Judiciary, Subcommittee to Investigate the
         Administration of the Internal Security Act and
         Other Internal Security Laws, <u>Institute of</u>
         <u>Pacific Relations, Part 13. Testimony of Igor</u>
         <u>Bogolepov</u>, 82nd Congress, 2nd Session, 1952,
         (Washington DC, GPO), pp. 4479-4520, 4479-
         4493.

480.   **U.S. CONGRESS, SENATE,** Committee on the
         Judiciary, Subcommittee to Investigate the
         Administration of the Internal Security Act and
         Other Internal Security Laws, <u>Espionage</u>
         <u>Activities of Personnel Attached to Embassies</u>
         <u>and Consulates in the U.S. Testimony of Matthew</u>
         <u>Cvetic, Joseph Ignac Molnar Jr., Pavline</u>
         <u>Svoboda</u>, 82nd Congress, 1st and 2nd Sessions,
         1951-1952, (Washington DC, GPO), pp. 1-52.

481.   **U.S. CONGRESS, SENATE,** Committee on the
         Judiciary, Subcommittee to Investigate the
         Administration of the Internal Security Act and
         Other Internal Security Laws, <u>Interlocking</u>
         <u>Subversion in Government Departments, Part 15.</u>
         <u>Testimony of Ismail Ege</u>, 83rd Congress, 1st
         Session, 1953, (Washington DC, GPO), pp.
         1001-1067.

482.   **U.S. CONGRESS, SENATE,** Committee on the
Judiciary, Subcommittee to Investigate the
Administration of the Internal Security Act and
Other Internal Security Laws, Activities of
Soviet Secret Service. Testimony of Nikolai
Evgeniyevich Khokhlov, 83rd Congress, 2nd
Session, 1954, (Washington DC, GPO), pp. 1-54.

483.   **U.S. CONGRESS, SENATE,** Committee on the
Judiciary, Subcommittee to Investigate the
Administration of the Internal Security Act and
Other Internal Security Laws. Testimony of
Former Russian Code Clerk Relating to the
Internal Security of the United States.
Testimony of Igor Gouzenko, 84th Congress, 1st
Session, 1955, (Washington DC, GPO), pp. 1-67.

484.   **U.S. CONGRESS, SENATE,** Committee on the
Judiciary, Subcommittee to Investigate the
Administration of the Internal Security Act and
Other Internal Security Laws, Scope of Soviet
Activity in the United States, Part 4. Testi-
mony of Mark Zborowsky, 84th Congress, 1st
Session, 1955, (Washington DC, GPO), pp.
77-101, 103-136.

485.   **U.S. CONGRESS, SENATE,** Committee on the
Judiciary, Subcommittee to Investigate the
Administration of the Internal Security Act and
Other Internal Security Laws, Scope of Soviet
Activity in the U.S., Parts 3 and 72. Testi-
mony of Ismail Ege (Lt. Col. Ismail Akhmedov),
84th Congress, 2nd Session, 1956, (Washington
DC, GPO), pp. 57-75, 4395-4398, 4404.

See also Ege's book In and Out of Stalin's GRU (q.v.).

486.   **U.S. CONGRESS, SENATE,** Committee on the
Judiciary, Subcommittee to Investigate the
Administration of the Internal Security Act and
Other Internal Security Laws, Scope of Soviet
Activity in the United States, Part 86.
Testimony of Nikolai Khokhlov, 84th Congress,
2nd Session, and 85th Congress, 1st Session,
1956-1957, (Washington DC, GPO), pp. 4818-
4841.

487. **U.S. CONGRESS, SENATE,** Committee on the Judiciary, Subcommittee to Investigate the Administration of the Internal Security Act and and Other Internal Security Laws, <u>Scope of Soviet Activity in the United States. Testimony of Yuri Rastvorov,</u> 84th Congress, 2nd Session, 1956, and 85th Congress, 1st Session, 1957, (Washington DC, GPO), pp. 1-23, 777-817, 3169-3176, 3334, 3335.

488. **U.S. CONGRESS, SENATE,** Committee on the Judiciary, Subcommittee to Investigate the Administration of the Internal Security Act and Other Internal Security Laws, <u>Scope of Soviet Activity in the United States, Part 51. Testimony of Alexander Orlov,</u> 85th Congress, 1st Session, 1957, (Washington DC, GPO), pp. 3421-3473.

489. **U.S. CONGRESS, SENATE,** Committee on the Judiciary, Subcommittee to Investigate the Administration of the Internal Security Act and Other Internal Security Laws, <u>Communist Controls on Religious Activity. Testimony of Peter S. Deriabin,</u> 86th Congress, 1st Session, 1959, (Washington DC, GPO), pp. 1-30. .

490. **U.S. CONGRESS, SENATE,** Committee on the Judiciary, Subcommittee to Investigate the Administration of the Internal Security Act and Other Internal Security Laws, <u>Soviet Intelligence in Asia. Testimony of Aleksandre Yurievich Kasnakheyev [Kaznacheyev],</u> 86th Congress, 1st Session, 1959, (Washington DC, GPO), pp. 1-25.

491. **U.S. CONGRESS, SENATE,** Committee on the Judiciary, Subcommittee to Investigate the Administration of the Internal Security Act and Other Internal Security Laws, <u>Conditions in the Soviet Union; The "New Class." Further Testimony of Aleksandre Y. Kasnakheyev [Kaznacheyev],</u> 86th Congress, 2nd Session, 1960, (Washington DC, GPO), pp. 1-38.

492. **U.S. CONGRESS, SENATE,** Committee on the
Judiciary, Subcommittee to Investigate the
Administration of the Internal Security Act and
Other Internal Security Laws, Soviet Espionage
Through Poland. Testimony of Pawel Monat, 86th
Congress, 2nd Session, 1960, (Washington DC,
GPO), pp. 1-39.

493. **U.S. CONGRESS, SENATE,** Committee on the Ju-
diciary, Subcommittee to Investigate the
Administration of the Internal Security Act and
Other Internal Security Laws, Expose of Soviet
Espionage- May 1960, prepared by the Federal
Bureau of Investigation, United States Depart-
ment of Justice, 86th Congress, 2nd Session,
1960, (Washington DC, GPO), pp. 1-63.

494. **U.S. CONGRESS, SENATE,** Committee on the Judiciary, Subcommittee to Investigate the
Administration of the Internal Security Act and
Other Internal Security Laws, The Pugwash
Conferences (Staff Analysis), 87th Congress,
1st Session, 1961, (Washington DC, GPO), pp.
1-139.

495. **U.S. CONGRESS, SENATE,** Committee on the
Judiciary, Subcommittee to Investigate the
Administration of the Internal Security Act and
Other Internal Security Laws, Communist
Forgeries. Testimony of Richard Helms,
Assistant Director, Central Intelligence
Agency, 87th Congress, 1st Session, 1961,
(Washington DC, GPO), pp. 1-115.

496. **U.S. CONGRESS, SENATE,** Committee on the
Judiciary, Subcommittee to Investigate the
Administration of the Internal Security Act and
Other Internal Security Laws, Communist
Penetration and Exploitation of a Free Press.
Testimony of Alesksandre Yurievich Kaznacheyev,
87th Congress, 2nd Session, 1962, (Washington
DC, GPO), pp. 16-21.

497. **U.S. CONGRESS, SENATE,** Committee on the
Judiciary, Subcommittee to Investigate the
Administration of the Internal Security Act and
Other Internal Security Laws. Testimony of
Alexander Orlov, 87th Congress, 2nd Session,
1962, (Washington DC, GPO), pp. 1-17.

These hearings, held in Executive Session in 1955, were not released until 1962.

498.　　**U.S. CONGRESS, SENATE,** Committee on the Judiciary, Subcommittee to Investigate the Administration of the Internal Security Act and Other Internal Security Laws, The Wennerstrom Spy Case, How it Touched the United States and NATO: Excerpts from the Testimony of Stig Eric Constans Wennerstrom, a Noted Soviet Agent, 88th Congress, 2nd Session, 1964, (Washington DC, GPO), pp. 166.

499.　　**U.S. CONGRESS, SENATE,** Committee on the Judiciary, Subcommittee to Investigate the Administration of the Internal Security Act and Other Internal Security Laws, Murder International Inc.: Murder and Kidnapping as an Instrument of Soviet Policy. Testimony of Peter S. Deriabin, 89th Congress, 1st Session, 1965, (Washington DC, GPO), pp. 168.

500.　　**U.S. CONGRESS, SENATE,** Committee on the Judiciary, Subcommittee to Investigate the Administration of the Internal Security Act and Other Internal Security Laws. Testimony of George Karlin (Yuri Krotkov), 91st Congress, 1st and 2nd Sessions, 1969 and 1970, in three Parts, (Washington DC, GPO), pp. 88, 166, and 258.

501.　　**U.S. CONGRESS, SENATE,** Committee on the Judiciary, Subcommittee to Investigate the Administration of the Internal Security Act and Other Internal Security Laws. Testimony of Col. Yevgeny Y. Runge, 91st Congress, 2nd Session, 1970, (Washington DC, GPO), pp. 64.

502.　　**U.S. CONGRESS, SENATE,** Committee on the Judiciary, Subcommittee to Investigate the Administration of the Internal Security Act and Other Internal Security Laws. Testimony of Lawrence Britt (Ladislav Bittman), 92nd Congress, 1st Session, 1971, (Washington DC, GPO), pp. 1-19.

503.   **U.S. CONGRESS, SENATE,** Committee on the
Judiciary, Subcommittee to Investigate the
Administration of the Internal Security Act and
Other Internal Security Laws. The Legacy of
Alexander Orlov, 93rd Congress, 1st Session,
1973, (Washington DC, GPO), pp. 150.

An in memoriam composite of Orlov's biography, Senate
testimony and his Life articles (q.v.).

504.   **U.S. CONGRESS, SENATE,** Committee on the
Judiciary, Subcommittee to Investigate the
Administration of the Internal Security Act and
Other Internal Security Laws, U.S.S.R. Labor
Camps. Testimony of Avraham Shifrin, 93rd
Congress, 1st Session, 1973, in three Parts,
(Washington DC, GPO), pp. 70, 128, 282.

505.   **U.S. CONGRESS, SENATE,** Committee on the
Judiciary, Subcommittee to Investigate the
Administration of the Internal Security Act and
Other Internal Security Laws, Communist Bloc
Intelligence Activities in the United States.
Testimony of Josef Frolik, 94th Congress, 1st
Session, pp. 64; 94th Congress, 2nd Session,
1976, Part 2, pp. 122, (Washington DC, GPO).

506.   **U.S. CONGRESS, SENATE,** Committee on the
Judiciary, Subcommittee on Security and
Terrorism, Historical Antecedents of Soviet
Terrorism, 96th Congress, 2nd Session, 1980,
(Washington DC, GPO), pp.1-33.

507.   **U.S. CONGRESS, SENATE,** Committee on the
Judiciary, Subcommittee on Security and
Terrorism, Communist Bloc Intelligence Gathering Activities on Capitol Hill, 97th Congress, 1st Session, 1981, (Washington DC, GPO),
pp. 67.

508.   **U.S. CONGRESS, SENATE, HOUSE,** Joint Committee
on Atomic Energy, Soviet Atomic Espionage, 82nd
Congress, 1st Session, 1951, (Washington DC,
GPO), pp. 222.

509.   **CENTRAL   INTELLIGENCE   AGENCY,** The Rote
        Kapelle: The CIA's History of Soviet Intel-
        ligence and Espionage Networks in Western
        Europe, 1935-1945, Washington, D.C.: University
        Publications of America, 1979, pp. 390.

A major work on the Rote Kapelle, including the Rote
Drei based in Switzerland, taken from official files.
Many members of these nets had been active in Soviet
intelligence in Europe for some years before World War
II. During the war years they were perhaps the principal Soviet sources of strategic military intelligence
about Germany.

510.   **CENTRAL INTELLIGENCE AGENCY,** Soviet Use of
        Assassination and Kidnapping, 7 February 1964,
        pp. 26.

This report, declassified by the CIA in January 1971,
was reprinted in, "The KGB Abroad. 'Wet Affairs',
Soviet Use of Assassination and Kidnapping". London,
England: Survey 27 (Autumn-Winter, 1983): pp. 68-79.
See also Warren Commission Files, US National Ar-
chives.

511.   **U.S. DEPARTMENT OF COMMERCE,** "Collection of
        Russian Articles on Soviet Intelligence and
        Security Operations".

        Translation available from National Technical
        Information Service, Springfield, Va., Order
        number: JPRS 55623, 4 April, 1972, pp. 229.

A very useful translation of 34 selected items from
Soviet books, journals, and newspapers. They reflect
the Soviet media projection of the new image of the
Soviet intelligence and security services, begun in the
early 1960s, covering the period 1962 to 1968.

512.   **U.S. DEPARTMENT OF JUSTICE,** Federal Bureau of
        Investigation, "Soviet Illegal Espionage in the
        United States", undated (circa 1957), pp. 35.

Deals with the Illegals, Reino Hayhanen and Rudolf
Abel.

513.   **U.S. DEPARTMENT OF JUSTICE**, Federal Bureau of
        Investigation, "Press Briefing...Col. Rudolph
        Herrman", 3 March 1980, pp. 5.

514.   **U.S. DEPARTMENT OF STATE**, Bureau of Public
        Affairs, "Report to the Congress on Forced
        Labor in the USSR", 9 February 1983, pp. 100.

515.   **U.S. DEPARTMENT OF STATE**, Bureau of Public
        Affairs, "Soviet Active Measures", Special
        Report Number 10, 1983, pp. 8.

516.   **U.S. DEPARTMENT OF STATE**, Bureau of Public
        Affairs, "Expulsions of Soviet Representatives
        from Foreign Countries, 1970-1981", Foreign
        Affairs Note, February 1982, pp. 8.

For updated coverage, see by the same source: Expulsions of Soviets Worldwide, 1982, January 1983, pp. 3,
and Expulsions of Soviets Worldwide, 1984, January
1985, pp. 3.

517.   **U.S. DEPARTMENT OF STATE**, Bureau of Public
        Affairs, "Soviet 'Active Measures': Forgery;
        Disinformation; Political Operations", Special
        Report No. 88, 1981, pp. 4.

518.   **U.S. DEPARTMENT OF STATE** , U.S. Information
        Service, "A Red Paper on Forced Labor [in the
        USSR]", 1952, pp. 69.

Appendix A

Glossary of Abbreviations and Terms

Cheka   Vserossiyskaya Chrezvychaynaya Komissiya po Borbe s Kontr Revolyutsiyey i Sabotazhem
All-Russian Extraordinary Commission to Combat Counterrevolution and Sabotage

GPU   Gosudarstvennoye Politicheskoye Upravleniye
State Political Directorate

OGPU   Obyedinennoye Gosudarstvennoye Politicheskoye Upravleniye
United State Political Directorate

NKVD   Narodnyy Komissariat Vnutrennikh Del
People's Commissariat of Internal Affairs

GUGB   Glavnoye Upravleniye Gosudarstvennoy Bezopasnosti
Chief Directorate (Main Administration) for State Security

NKGB   Narodnyy Komissariat Gosudarstvennoy Bezopasnosti
People's Commissariat of State Security

Smersh   "Smert Shpionam" - "Death to Spies"
Popular title of Armed Forces Counterintelligence Directorate, 1943-46

KI   Komitet Informatsii
Committee of Information

MVD   Ministerstvo Vnutrenikh Del
Ministry of Internal Affairs

MGB   Ministerstvo Gosudarstvennoy Bezopasnosti
Ministry of State Security

KGB   Komitet Gosudarstvennoy Bezopasnosti
Committee for State Security

MOOP   Ministerstvo Okhrany Obshchestvennogo Poryadka
Ministry for Maintenance of Public Order

GRU   Glavnoye Razvedyvatelnoye Upravleniye
Main Intelligence Directorate
(of General Staff)

Appendix B

KGB Leadership

1917-26	Feliks Dzerzhinskiy
1926-34	Vyacheslav Menzhinskiy
1934-36	Genrikh Yagoda
1936-38	Nikolay Yezhov
1938-46	Lavrentiy Beriya (with Vsevolod Merkulov from 1941)
1946(Jan) - 1946(Mar)	Sergey Kruglov
1946(Mar) - 1946(Oct)	Vsevolod Merkulov
1946(Oct) - 1951(Aug)	Viktor Abakumov
1951(Aug) - 1951(Dec?)	Sergey Ogoltsov (Acting Chief)
1951(Dec?)- 1953(Mar)	Semyon Ignatyev
1953(Mar) - 1953(June)	Lavrentiy Beriya
1953-54	Sergey Kruglov
1954-58	Ivan Serov
1958-61	Aleksandr Shelepin
1961-67	Vladimir Semichastnyy
1967-82	Yuriy Andropov
1982(May) - 1982(Dec)	Vitaliy Fedorchuk
1982 -	Viktor Chebrikov

Appendix C

GRU Leadership

1918-24	Not positively identified
1924-35	General Yan Berzin
1935-37	General S. P. Uritskiy
1937	General Yan Berzin
1937-38	Nikolai Yezhov (concurrently Chief of NKVD)
1938-40	Lt. General Ivan Proskurov
1940-41	General Filip Golikov
1941-43	General Aleskandr Panfilov
1942-43	General Ivan Ilichev
1943-47	General Fydor Kuznetsov
1947-48	Part of Committee of Information (KI)
1948-50	General Vladimir Kurasov
1950-51	General Matvey Zakharov
1951-56	General Mikhail Shalin
1956-57	General Sergey Shtemenko
1957-58	General Mikhail Shalin
1958-63	General Ivan Serov
1963-	General Petr Ivashutin

Development of Soviet Intelligence & Security Services

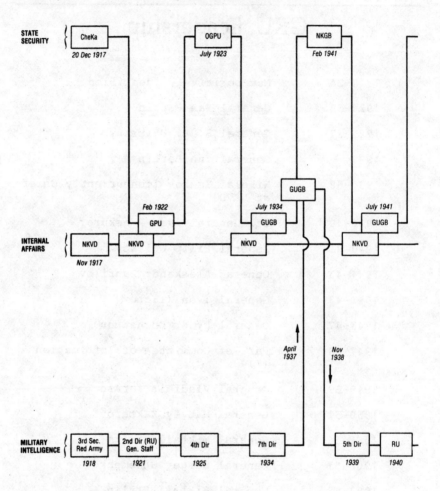

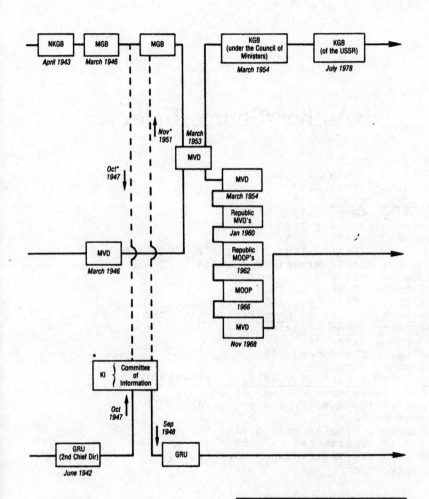

KI, under the Council of Ministers & headed by the Foreign Minister absorbed MGB external functions *only*, from Oct 1947 to Nov 1951; and GRU intelligence functions from Oct 1947 to Sep 1948

Author/Source Index

Title Index